THE COOKING OF EMILIA-ROMAGNA

THE COOKING OF EMILIA-ROMAGNA

Culinary Treasures from Northern Italy

GIOVANNA BELLIA LA MARCA

HIPPOCRENE BOOKS, INC.
New York

Also by Giovanna Bellia La Marca:

Sicilian Feasts

Language & Travel Guide to Sicily

Illustrated edition, 2025

Copyright © 2025, 2011 Giovanna Bellia La Marca.

All rights reserved.

Color photographs by Francesca LaMarca Sacco.

Jacket design by Acme Klong Design.

For more information, address:
HIPPOCRENE BOOKS, INC.
171 Madison Avenue
New York, NY 10016
www.hippocrenebooks.com

Cataloging-in-Publication Data available from the Library of Congress

Previous edition ISBN: 978-0-7818-1256-6

Printed in the United States of America.

DEDICATION

This book is dedicated to the memory of our beloved Aunt Elvira Franceschini Riggi who brought the cooking of Emilia-Romagna to the United States, and to her niece Annamaria Clerici, who continued her family traditions by creating culinary wonders in her tiny kitchen in their native town of Berceto.

ACKNOWLEDGMENTS

I thank Annemaria Clerici for all that I've learned from her during our many visits to Berceto and in frequent phone conversations while I tested recipes in Cliffside Park. Thanks for the wonderful stories and chestnut recipes that Mariolina Grassi and her sons Gianni and Giorgio shared with me over the years. My thanks to Mark and Isabella Musa for sharing family recipes and to the Musa and Berni families for introducing my husband Howard to the cooking of the region of Parma from the time he met Mark in the first grade. I am most grateful to Laura Berni for sharing with me her mother Angiolina's treasured handwritten notebook of traditional recipes.

My thanks to my family for their continued support: To my husband, Howard, for his daily help; to our daughter, Nicoletta La Marca Sacco, for bringing sunshine into our lives; to our son-in-law, Dr. Steven Christopher Sacco, for his affection; to our grandson Felice for being our resident computer techie; and to our granddaughter Francesca for her infectious laughter which keeps the entire family in good humor.

CONTENTS

EMILIA-ROMAGNA

INTRODUCTION

Since Italian cooking is based on the products of the region, none is more fortunate than Emilia-Romagna, which counts among its culinary miracles the world-renowned Prosciutto di Parma, Parmigiano Reggiano cheese, considered the king of cheeses, and the flavorful dried porcini mushrooms of Borgo Val Di Taro. The region includes the very fertile Po Valley and the Apennine mountains, with enchanting hill towns dotting the landscape finally ending in the Adriatic Sea.

The region produces the soft wheat that is ideal for the fresh, rich egg pasta which is the centerpiece of its famous cooking. This is the region where noodles, such as *tagliatelle*, lasagne, and filled pasta dishes, like *tortellini* in broth and *tortelli* (a type of ravioli) served with sauce, are the stars of the table. The savory fillings of the various kinds of *tortelli* are made with the cured meats for which this area is known. *Culatello*, the cured inner part of the ham that is another specialty of Parma and even more prized than prosciutto, is fantastic on a piece of *gnocco fritto* or fried dough as an appetizer with a glass of lambrusco, the favored wine of the region. A cured specialty from the city of Modena is *zampone*, stuffed pig's foot, which is a must for the traditional New Year's Day dinner accompanied by lentils and mashed potatoes.

Emilia-Romagna is made up of what were historically two distinct areas. Emilia's cities, Piacenza, Parma, Reggio Emilia, and Bologna, follow each other along the ancient Roman road named Via Emilia. The territory of Romagna, that includes the cities of Ferrara, Ravenna, Forli' and Rimini, is bound by the Adriatic Sea. The cooking of Emilia derives from a cooking tradition of sumptuous yet delicate foods. The cooking of Romagna is traditionally robust, with more assertive flavors, pairing well with the Sangiovese wine favored in the region. Of course being bound by the Adriatic Sea, the meats of Emilia give way to the bounty of the sea.

Bologna, the capital of the region, is known as "*la dotta*" or "the learned" because of its ancient university which was established in 1088 as the first in Europe and in the Italic peninsula (as the geographic location was known long before the regions were united in 1861 into the sovereign country of Italy). This beautiful northern city is known for its miles of elegant porticoed streets, its great museums, and of course, its still outstanding university. Near the university are Bologna's own pair of leaning towers: La Garisenda and La Torre Degli Asinelli, that stand as symbols of the city. The art museum known as the Pinacoteca Nazionale, housed in a Renaissance palace, surprises the visitor with its modern interior, indirect lighting, and beautifully designed displays. Music lovers will be delighted to visit the Museo Civico Musicale that has a vast collection of manuscripts and scores dating from before 1900, together with a collection of instruments and a gallery of portraits.

Bologna has yet another distinction: it's also called "*la grassa*" (literally meaning fat) from the days when the use of fat in cooking was a good thing and a sign of wealth, taste, pride, and family well-being. This is a city where everyone eats well, even a traveler just passing through its train station. Although you can get wonderful lunch boxes packed with the local specialties and a bottle of wine or water in every Italian railroad station, in Bologna the lunch is likely to include the choice of hot *Lasagne Bolognesi*, the delicious freshly made spinach noodles layered with the traditional Bolognese sauce and creamy white béchamel sauce, then liberally sprinkled with grated Parmigiano-Reggiano and dotted with butter. Rich and delicate at the same time, this dish is one of the stars of Italian cooking.

To the north of Bologna, the city of Modena is known for its exceptional balsamic vinegar, which has taken the culinary world by storm. Modena's Romanesque cathedral stands as a testament to the work of human genius. This medieval complex, begun in 1099, has been named a UNESCO World Heritage site because of the singular manner in which architecture and sculpture are integrated to serve both religious and secular needs.

The city of Parma needs no introduction as a culinary nirvana. It is known throughout the world for its Prosciutto di Parma, a distinctive cured ham of exceptional flavor, and for Parmigiano, long regarded as the king of cheeses and sold as Parmigiano-Reggiano. The city was governed by the beloved Maria Luisa Duchess of Parma, the second wife of Napoleon, from 1815 to 1847, a period of peace and prosperity. One fragrant symbol of the city are *Violette di Parma* which were once made into a perfume for Maria Luisa and continue to be the favorite traditional scent. The Cathedral of Parma has a beautiful and very unusual medieval baptistery dating back to the twelfth century that was designed by the master sculptor and architect Benedetto Antelami in a unique octagonal shape that allows for baptism by immersion. Parma's Teatro Regio, in a city that has a major music conservatory, boasts one of the most discriminating and demanding opera audiences; a natural since Emilia-Romagna has given the world

Giuseppe Verdi, Arturo Toscanini, Mirella Freni, and Luciano Pavarotti.

The city of Ferrara, built on the delta of the Po River to the east of Parma, is another UNESCO World Heritage site. This city exemplifies the Renaissance humanist concept of the "ideal city" designed and built according to the then-new principles of perspective, making it the birthplace of modern town planning. The magnificent decorations of the Palazzi d'Este by Jacopo Bellini, Piero Della Francesca, and Andrea Mantegna attest to Ferrara's place as a Renaissance center of artistic and intellectual geniuses.

The first time we went to the mountain town of Bedonia, we experienced first-hand the beauty, the generous hospitality, and the incomparable cuisine of the region. We were on our honeymoon visiting my husband's best friend, Mark Musa, who was spending the summer with his parents, together with his beautiful wife Isabella. Our welcome dinner, prepared by Cleonige, the family housekeeper and cook, introduced us to *malfatti*, a dumpling made from the spinach and ricotta filling usually used to fill the equally delicious *tortelli* (a kind of ravioli). *Malfatti*, which literally means "badly made," are balls of spinach, ricotta, Parmigiano, and egg that are coated with flour, poached, and dressed with melted butter. This delectable and easy to make dish immediately became and has remained to this day our very favorite Italian *primo* or first course. Isabella also treated us to *Bomba di Riso*, an oven-baked molded rice dish from her native Parma that is another outstanding typical dish of the region. (An amusing side note: Cleonige had been with the family forever and took great pride in her cooking and housekeeping. She was so insulted when an American washing machine arrived in Bedonia that she refused to use it. On subsequent trips we could see the still brand-new washing machine languishing in a corner covered with a sheet.)

Berceto, another beautiful hill town and the birthplace of our beloved Aunt Elvira, seems to have everything: the remains of an ancient castle, a stately medieval duomo, picturesque panoramas, and some of the finest restaurants in the region. Dining at the nationally known restaurant Da Rino in the center of town was always an exceptional experience. Treats such as *Torta Fritta* (page 13) and appetizing mushroom dishes expertly prepared in literally dozens of different ways were the rule.

The town of Bardi also has its own castle that has been fully restored and is open to the public. A culinary curiosity of this town rests with the fact that many of the people of Bardi emigrated to England, and return for their vacations, so the local cafés serve tea and sherry in the afternoon.

Our friend Irene Berni often made her special *Torta Bianca di Mandorle* (page 152), a white almond cake that she served with afternoon tea in her lovely villa.

Continuing on the Via Emilia towards the sea, we come to Ravenna, another World Heritage site for the fifth- and sixth-century basilicas of Sant'Apollinare Nuovo and Sant'Apollinare in Classe, which together with the medieval church of San Vitale exhibit some of the most extraordinary mosaics in the world. My visit to Ravenna remains memorable since I arrived on August 15th or *Ferragosto*, a day when Italian cities are entrusted to the travelers while the Italians flock to the countryside, the mountains, or the seashore. It was a magical day. Empty of most of its inhabitants—with practically no traffic and certainly no buses or taxis—walking around this beautiful medieval city I felt transported in time. I brought flowers to the tomb of Dante Alighieri who ended his days exiled in Ravenna.

In Riccione, we reach the Adriatic Riviera with its sandy beaches, spirited nightlife, and outstanding fish dishes, including the exceptional *Brodetto Romagnolo*, a rich and flavorful fish soup/stew second to none.

This magnificent region, with the natural beauty of its green valleys, imposing mountains, and seaside resorts is not only rich in history, art, and traditions, but it takes pride in having one of the great cuisines of Italy. It is said that all other regions of Italy acknowledge that the cooking of Emilia-Romagna is at least as good as their own.

APPETIZERS AND SNACKS

Antipasti e Stuzzichini

Antipasti are the welcome beginnings of festive meals throughout the year and are also generally served when we entertain guests at home. *Stuzzichini* are snacks enjoyed at different times of day, perhaps to accompany a glass of wine or just to share with family and friends. The *antipasti* of Emilia-Romagna are savory *assaggini* (little bites) that are meant to whet the appetite, never to satisfy it.

A wealth of cured meats, such as prosciutto, *culatello*, *salame*, and mortadella accompanied by the incomparable *piadine* (the traditional flat bread of Romagna), *torta fritta* (the fried flat bread of the Parma region), *tigelle* (little muffins made in and around the city of Modena and grilled on top of the stove), or *borlengo* (a large pancake brushed with a savory condiment and folded into quarters), are delicious accents before the main event, which for Emilia Romagna is the fresh pasta. Of course, these delicious savories can be enjoyed as *merende* (afternoon snacks) by children who look forward to their *panino con mortadella* (mortadella sandwich) after school. Other times, they become the meal itself, as a lovely platter of meats accompanied by a basket of fresh breads is often served as a light supper with an accompanying salad or *verdura* (cooked greens) and crowned by the classic finale—chunks of Parmigiano-Reggiano cheese and fresh fruit.

ANTIPASTI E STUZZICHINI
APPETIZERS AND SNACKS

BEEF CARPACCIO

Carpaccio di Manzo

Serves 12 to 16 or more in a buffet

The term* carpaccio *means that the fresh meat is salted, sprinkled with pepper, and seared on the outside to keep the juices in, but not cooked. The thin slices are then seasoned for additional flavor. Although originally prepared with beef tenderloin, the term has become generic for a thinly sliced meat or fish seasoned with a savory sauce.

- 1-pound piece center-cut beef tenderloin
- 1 teaspoon coarse salt
- 1 teaspoon coarse freshly ground black pepper
- Extra virgin olive oil
- Balsamic vinegar
- Arugula leaves for garnish
- shavings of Parmigiano-Reggiano cheese

Coat the tenderloin liberally with salt and pepper. Heat the olive oil in a small frying pan that will fit the meat snugly. When very hot, add the meat and quickly sear on all sides over high heat. (This is meant to make a thin, flavorful crust on the tenderloin not to cook the meat.) Cool the meat and place in the freezer for 45 to 60 minutes to make it possible to slice the meat paper thin.

Remove the seared tenderloin from the freezer and immediately slice it paper-thin. Gently press the slices with a *batticarne* (meat pounder) to make them as thin as possible. Arrange the slices of meat in a single layer on one or two large platters, sprinkle with salt, and drizzle with your best extra virgin olive oil and balsamic vinegar. Garnish the platters with arugula leaves. Before serving, top the carpaccio with shaved Parmigiano-Reggiano cheese.

WHITE TRUFFLES AND MUSHROOMS
FUNGHI E TARTUFI BIANCHI

Possibly the most luxurious food in the world, the white truffles of Emilia-Romagna are among the most fragrant. On your next fall trip to Bologna, savor the experience of enjoying thinly sliced truffle on *tagliatelle*, fresh egg noodles, eggs, or served with a drizzle of extra virgin olive oil, a pinch of salt, and a touch of lemon, but meanwhile, buy a truffle slicer and use it for fresh mushrooms to make a delicious antipasto.

MARINATED MUSHROOMS
Funghi Marinati

Serves 4 to 6 or more in a buffet

6 ounces fresh white button or cremini mushrooms
¼ cup extra virgin olive oil
juice of one lemon
salt and pepper to taste

Remove the stems from the mushrooms and reserve for soups or stews. Clean the caps and slice very thinly. Toss gently with the very best available extra virgin olive oil and the lemon juice and sprinkle with salt and pepper. Let stand to marinate until ready to serve.

SAUTÉED MUSHROOMS *Funghi Trifolati*

Serves 4 to 6 or more in a buffet

- 1 tablespoon dried porcini mushrooms
- ¼ cup extra virgin olive oil
- 1 clove garlic
- 1 pound mushrooms (a mixture of button, cremini, portobello, chanterelle, and/or shitake), trimmed, cleaned, and sliced
- ½ teaspoon salt
- freshly ground black pepper
- 2 tablespoons butter
- ½ cup chopped Italian flat-leaf parsley

Soak the dried porcini mushrooms in ¼ cup warm water for 15 minutes. Lift the dried mushrooms from the soaking water with a slotted spoon (reserving the water), wash carefully and chop.

Heat the olive oil in a medium skillet. Add the garlic clove and remove when it begins to color. Add the soaked porcini mushrooms to the garlic-flavored oil, stir, then add the sliced mushrooms and stir to mix. Cook for 3 minutes, stirring from time to time.

Filter the reserved mushroom water through a fine sieve right into the pan with the mushrooms, add salt and pepper and continue to cook, uncovered, until the liquid has evaporated. Turn off the heat, add the butter and stir; then add the parsley and stir again.

PROSCIUTTO

Prosciutto di Parma is an exceptionally delicious ham that has made its city of origin justly famous for the incomparable flavor of this world famous treat. Although generally served in small portions as an antipasto, I remember to this day a very special lunch featuring an abundant platter of expertly hand-cut prosciutto, excellent freshly baked bread still warm from the oven, and a green salad perfectly dressed with fragrant extra virgin olive oil, salt, and a touch of balsamic vinegar. This was lunch on the road, and we enjoyed it in a favorite trattoria when my cousin Felice Muccio and I drove from Milano to Riccione by way of Parma.

PROSCIUTTO AND MELON

Prosciutto e Melone

6 servings

This is a classic combination. But also try the variation of using fresh figs in place of the melon when they're available.

- 12 slices cantaloupe or honeydew melon
- 12 slices prosciutto di Parma

Drape slices of freshly cut prosciutto di Parma on slices of fragrant cantaloupe.

PROSCIUTTO AND ASPARAGUS

Prosciutto e Asparagi

6 servings

- 18 stalks asparagus
- 18 slices prosciutto di Parma

Trim the asparagus, place in a square glass pan, cover with boiling water, let stand for 5 minutes. Drain and cool.

Wrap each asparagus stalk with a slice of prosciutto. Arrange attractively on a platter and serve.

PROSCIUTTO ON ITALIAN BREADSTICKS

Prosciutto e Grissini

6 servings

- 18 Grissini or Italian breadsticks
- 18 slices prosciutto di Parma

Wrap each breadstick with a slice of prosciutto. Arrange attractively on a platter and serve.

MIXED APPETIZER
Antipasto Misto

6 to 8 servings

Although we tend to think of Parmigiano-Reggiano as a grating cheese, it's a delicious table cheese and a wonderful addition to an antipasto platter. Elsa Peretti, the world-famous Italian-born designer of silver flatware and silver and gold jewelry, created a special silver parmigiano knife for Tiffany and Company, which when placed next to a wedge of this king of cheeses presents it in truly grand style on the buffet or dining table! My husband and I love to give the Elsa Peretti parmigiano knife accompanied by a lovely piece of cheese as a wedding gift. Her beautiful silver knife from Tiffany graces the cover of this book.

- ¼ pound prosciutto di Parma
- ½ pound salame
- ½ pound mortadella
- chunks of Parmigiano-Reggiano cheese

Arrange thin slices of prosciutto on a platter, overlap rounds of salame and slices of mortadella folded into quarters. Add chunks of Parmigiano-Reggiano to enjoy with the delicious *salumi* (Italian cold cuts) for a wonderfully appetizing antipasto.

Accompany with crusty bread, *grissini*, *piadina* (page 14), *tigelle* (page 18), or *torta fritta* (also known as *gnocco fritto*, page 13).

FRUIT SKEWERS WITH SAPA

Spiedini con Sapa

Serves 6 to 8 as an antipasto or many more at a party

Sapa *is an ancient condiment made by reducing grape must flavored with cinnamon, cloves, and lemon zest to thicken it and concentrate the flavor.*

8 ounces Parmigiano-Reggiano cheese, broken into small chunks

8 ounces seedless grapes

8 ounces strawberries, washed

4 ounces *sapa*

4-inch decorative toothpicks

Skewer one grape, a piece of Parmigiano-Reggiano, and a strawberry on each toothpick. Change the order on the next one to strawberry, cheese, and grape. Continue until all fruit and cheese is used.

To serve as *aperitivi* at a dinner, place 3 to 5 skewers on a small plate, drizzle *sapa* over all of them, and serve.

For a party, wrap a boiled potato in aluminum foil, place in a pretty footed bowl and stick the skewers into the potato so that guests can serve themselves. Serve the *sapa* in a small bowl as a dipping sauce.

PRESERVED FRUITS
MOSTARDA

Although *mostarda* sounds like *mustard*, these words are false friends because *mostarda* is fruit cooked in *mosto* (wine must) not in mustard which in Italian is called *senape*. *Mostarda* is used in the preparation of desserts and ravioli and as a condiment when serving *bollito misto* (mixed boiled dinner, page 96) or *cotechino* (the delicious sweet sausage of Emilia-Romagna traditionally served on New Year's Day). *Mostarda* is readily available in Italian Markets.

DIAMONDS OF FRIED DOUGH

Torta Fritta

8 to 12 servings

High in the Apennine mountains the beautiful town of Berceto boasts three fabulous restaurants. When the original owner welcomed his guests at his renowned restaurant Da Rino, on the main street in town up the street from the beautiful twelfth-century duomo, a basket of hot torta fritta *would be served with the antipasto to whet your appetite.*

- 1 tablespoon dry yeast
- 1 cup warm water
- 3½ cups all-purpose flour
- 1 teaspoon salt
- 1 tablespoon lard, butter, or shortening
- 1 teaspoon olive oil
- 2 to 3 cups canola oil for deep frying

Dissolve the yeast in the warm water and let stand for a few minutes to proof.

Mix the flour and salt and rub in the lard or butter until well distributed. Add the yeast mixture and mix into a dough. Knead briefly, shape into a ball, coat with a teaspoon of olive oil and let rise for one hour or until doubled.

Divide the dough into 2 portions. Roll out each portion to ¼-inch thickness, cut into 1½-inch strips and then cut the strips at an angle into diamond shapes.

Heat canola oil in a deep pot. Deep fry the dough diamonds in the hot oil until lightly browned on both sides. Drain on paper towels and dust with a little sprinkle of salt.

GRILLED FLAT BREAD
Piadina

8 to 12 servings

This delicious flat unleavened bread is one of the ancient breads of the Romagna region. Traditionally cooked on a testo *(an earthenware grill over a charcoal fire), they are now baked in a cast-iron griddle pan on top of the stove. Although lard is the traditional fat of choice, and it gives the best flavor, it can be substituted completely or in part with butter or vegetable shortening with equal success. Lard, which is not less healthful or more caloric than butter, does make a tastier* piadina*, so if you don't have dietary restrictions don't be afraid to try lard as an alternative to butter. Of course, use either in moderation.*

- 3 cups all-purpose flour
- ½ teaspoon salt
- ¼ teaspoon baking soda
- ½ cup lard, butter, or shortening
- ¾ cup water

NOTE: To serve *piadina* as a delicious snack, spread with soft cheese such as squaquaron, stracchino, mascarpone, or even American cream cheese, top with a slice of prosciutto and cooked greens such as cabbage, spinach, or swiss chard (recipes given on the next two pages), fold in half and eat while still warm.

Mix flour, salt, and baking soda. Cut the lard into the mixture until it resembles coarse crumbs. Add the water and mix into a medium stiff dough.

Divide the dough into 2 portions. Roll each portion into a rope and cut into 8 pieces. Shape each piece into a ball, then take each ball of dough, coat lightly with flour to keep from sticking, and roll into a thin disk. Place the disks between squares of wax or parchment paper until you are ready to cook them.

Heat a cast-iron griddle on top of the stove, place one of the rolled out disks of dough on the griddle, turn often and prick with a fork to keep flat until the two sides are flecked with brown. Stack the breads on a platter and cover with a towel to keep warm while cooking the remaining bread.

SAVOY CABBAGE ROMAGNA-STYLE

Cavoli alla Romagnola

8 to 12 servings

medium head savoy cabbage

4 tablespoons butter

1 onion, sliced

salt and pepper to taste

Cut the cabbage in half, remove the core, wash, and blanch in a pot of boiling salted water for 5 minutes. Drain, cool, chop the cabbage and set aside.

Heat the butter in a medium skillet, add the onion and cook until softened. Add the cabbage, salt, and pepper to taste and cook for 15 to 20 minutes, stirring often and adding water if needed 1 tablespoon at a time until the cabbage is fragrant and it begins to lightly brown. Serve at room temperature as a filling for the *piadina* (opposite page).

WILTED SPINACH

Spinaci Saltati

8 to 12 servings

2 10-ounce bags fresh spinach, trimmed and washed

4 tablespoons butter

1 clove garlic

salt and freshly ground pepper to taste

Remove the tough stems from the spinach. Wash in a bowl of water and lift the spinach out with whatever water the leaves retain.

Heat the butter in a medium skillet, add the clove of garlic and cook until fragrant. Remove the clove of garlic or mash it and leave it in, if desired. Add the spinach, salt and pepper to taste, cover the pan and cook for 10 minutes, stirring from time to time. Serve warm on *piadina* (opposite page).

STIR-FRIED SWISS CHARD
Bietole Saltate

8 to 12 servings

1 or 2 bunches Swiss chard (4 cups chopped)

4 tablespoons butter

1 clove garlic

salt and freshly ground pepper to taste

Trim the Swiss chard, separate the stems from the leaves and wash. Blanch the stems in boiling salted water for 5 minutes. Drain, cool, and cut in ½-inch slices. Chop the leaves coarsely and set aside.

Heat the butter in a medium skillet, add the clove of garlic and cook until fragrant. Remove the garlic or mash it and leave it in, if desired. Add the chopped Swiss chard stems with ¼ cup water, cover the pan and cook for 10 minutes, stirring from time to time. Add the chopped Swiss chard leaves, salt and pepper to taste, and continue to cook uncovered and stirring often for another 10 minutes. Serve warm on *piadina* (page 14).

PINZIMONIO

6 to 8 servings

This is an olive oil dip for crunchy vegetables: slices of red, green and/or yellow bell peppers; cucumber sticks; fennel slices; celery sticks; tender leaves of Romaine lettuce; scallions; radishes; blanched artichoke hearts.

½ cup extra virgin olive oil

¼ cup balsamic vinegar

salt to taste

Mix the olive oil and balsamic vinegar in a small bowl and add salt to taste. Place in the center of a serving platter with your choice of vegetables attractively arranged around it. Place the platter on a lazy susan for easy reach of the people around the table.

FRIED ZUCCHINI STICKS

Zucchini Fritti

Serves 4 to 6 or more in a buffet

Elvira Fanceschini Riggi came from the province of Parma and continued to cook the traditional dishes of her native Berceto, a picturesque small town built on the side of a mountain. Aunt Elvira often prepared this dish because it was our daughter Nicoletta's favorite. Nicoletta now remembers Zia Elvira as she makes this family favorite for her husband and children.

- 2 zucchini, unpeeled but well scrubbed
- 2 eggs, beaten
- ½ teaspoon salt
- ¼ teaspoon freshly ground black pepper
- 1 cup all-purpose flour
- ½ cup canola oil for frying

Cut each of the zucchini into 8 long wedges. Beat the eggs with the salt and pepper.

Coat the zucchini wedges lightly with flour, shaking off the excess, dip in the egg, and then give them another coat of flour. Set aside until ready to fry.

Preheat the oven to 200 degrees. Heat the oil in a large frying pan, add the zucchini taking care that they not touch. Brown on all sides. Drain on paper towels and place in the 200-degree oven to keep warm until all are cooked.

LITTLE STOVE-TOP MUFFINS WITH SAVORY SPREAD

Tigelle con Condimento

8 to 12 servings

Tigelle *are a delicious specialty of the mountains near Modena. They are not baked in the oven, but instead cooked on top of the stove. Traditionally they were sandwiched between hot tiles so that the top and bottom of the little breads cooked at the same time. In Italy there are hinged pans that cook anywhere from 2 to 12* tigelle *sandwiched between two metal plates on top of the stove, but a cast-iron griddle pan works well. They are served hot, split and spread with* condimento. *(But don't be scandalized if someone spreads Nutella on the hot* tigelle *as does our nine-year-old granddaughter Francesca!)*

1 tablespoon dry yeast
1 cup warm water
3 cups all-purpose flour
1 teaspoon salt
2 tablespoons soft lard, butter, or shortening

CONDIMENTO:

4 ounces Italian lardo, salt pork fatback, or pancetta, very finely minced
1 clove fresh garlic, finely minced
½ teaspoon fresh rosemary leaves, minced
¼ cup freshly grated Parmigiano-Reggiano cheese

Mince all the ingredients for the *condimento* by hand or give them a few pulses in the food processor to reduce everything to a paste. Spoon into a small bowl and set aside.

Dissolve the yeast in the warm water and let stand for a few minutes to proof.

Mix the flour and salt and rub in the lard or butter until well distributed. Add the yeast mixture and mix into a dough. Knead briefly, shape into a ball, coat with a teaspoon of olive oil and let rise for one hour or until doubled.

Divide dough into 2 pieces. Roll each piece on a lightly floured board to a ½-inch thick rectangle. Using a glass or a 2-inch biscuit cutter, cut as many circles as you can. Take the scraps of dough, add them to the second piece and roll out and cut as above. Place the dough circles on a towel, cover and let rise for about 30 minutes.

Preheat the oven to 200 degrees. Heat a cast-iron griddle pan, brush with a little olive oil and cook the *tigelle* over medium heat, turning them often until they are speckled with golden spots on both sides (if the spots turn black, the heat is too high). Keep them warm in the 200-degree oven until ready to serve.

Split the *tigelles*, spread ½ teaspoon of *condimento* on each one, and enjoy with a glass of Sangiovese wine, the traditional favorite of Romagna.

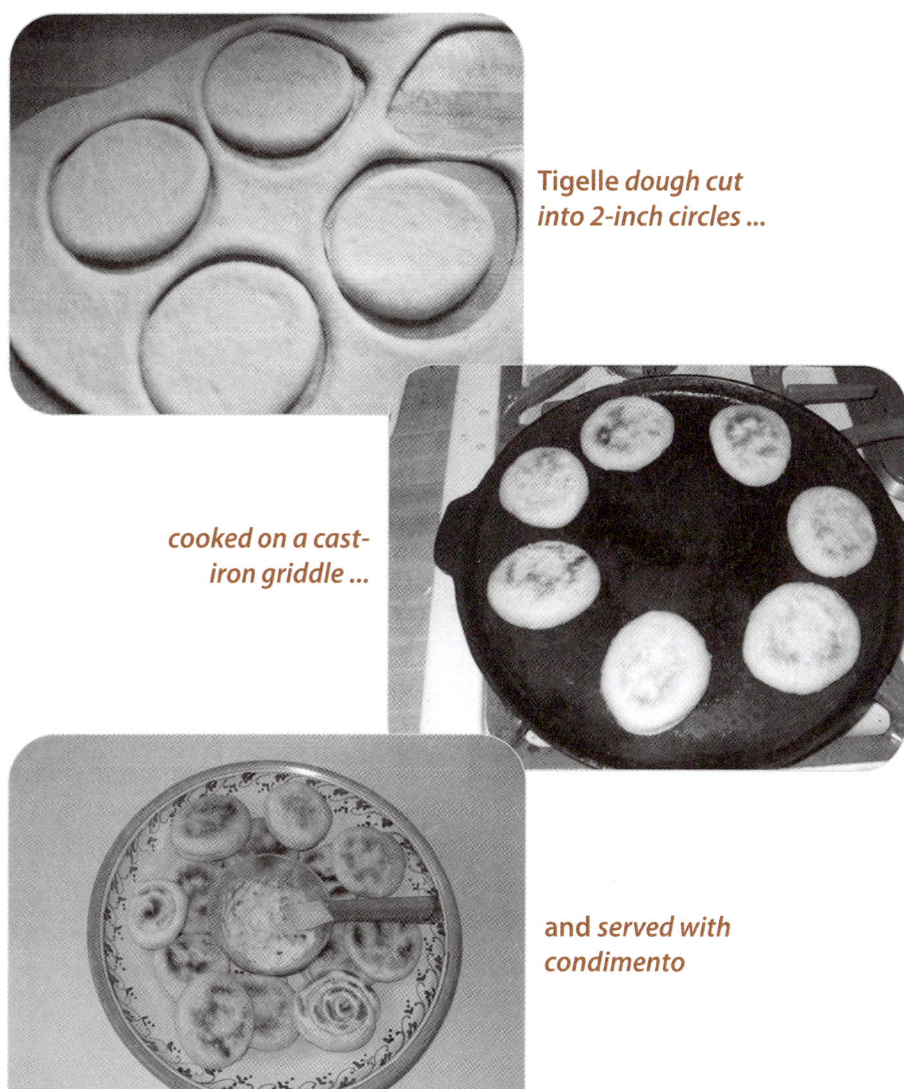

Tigelle *dough cut into 2-inch circles ...*

cooked on a cast-iron griddle ...

and *served with condimento*

SAVORY PANCAKE WITH SAVORY SPREAD

Borlengo con Condimento

4 to 6 servings

In and near the city of Modena, a gathering of friends, a hot rola *(a* borlengo *pan with a 24-inch diameter), a bowl of* colla *(the name of the batter), and a freshly opened bottle of Lambrusco were the traditional makings of a party with minimum expense and maximum pleasure.* Borlengo *is a real treat all on its own. Recently featured in the* New York Times *by Florence Fabricant, who even gave the recipe from the restaurant Via Emilia in Manhattan, this crisp yet soft flat bread encloses a savory* condimento *similar to the kind used for* tigelle, *but since it's spread on the* borlengo *while it's still in the pan, it has a chance to melt before the* borlengo *is topped with a generous dusting of Parmigiano and then folded into quarters. Chef Owner William Mattiello makes each to order using the* rola *especially made for him in Modena.*

2 eggs
½ teaspoon salt
1 cup all-purpose flour
4 ounces (1 cup) freshly grated Parmigiano-Reggiano cheese for topping

CONDIMENTO:

4 ounces Italian lardo, salt-cured pork fatback, or pancetta, very finely minced (½ cup extra virgin olive oil can be substituted)
1 clove fresh garlic, finely minced
½ teaspoon fresh rosemary leaves, minced

Make a batter with the eggs, salt, flour and ¾ cup of water, and let stand for 30 minutes.

Mince all the ingredients for the *condimento* by hand or give them a few pulses in the food processor to reduce everything to a paste. Set aside.

Lightly rub a nonstick 10-inch pan with a piece of prosciutto rind or brush with a film of vegetable oil. Using a scant ¼ cup of batter, make a thin pancake and brown on one sides. Turn it, spread a teaspoon of *condimento* on the *borlengo,* and allow it to melt and the other side to brown. Dust generously with freshly grated Parmigiano-Reggiano, fold into quarters and serve. Repeat with remaining batter.

A borlengo *topped with a snowfall of Parmigiano-Reggiano before folding into quarters ...*

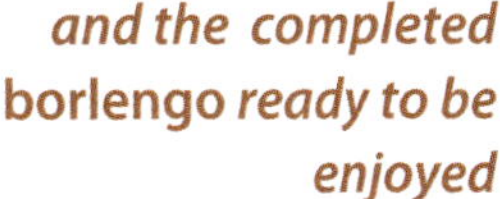

and the completed borlengo *ready to be enjoyed*

DOUGH FOR TORTE (SAVORY PIES)
Pasta Matta

Makes enough dough for 1 torta

The dough for torte *is called* pasta matta *which means "crazy dough," so called because it's only made with flour, olive oil, and milk without the enrichment of butter and eggs. Crazy as it might seem, it holds its shape just like the fancier dough. My friend from Berceto, Annamaria Clerici, rolls the dough for* torte *in a pasta machine, stopping just before the thinnest size; she then overlaps the strips and presses them together with her finger tips to join them together before cutting a large circle that overhangs the pan by about 2 inches. If the* torta *requires a top crust she cuts the remaining strips into thin ribbons with a fluted pastry wheel and places them criss-crossed on top of the filling before folding the edge of the dough over the top.*

2½ cups all-purpose flour
½ teaspoon salt
¼ cup extra virgin olive oil
½ cup milk
Glaze: 1 beaten egg

Mix the flour and salt. Add the olive oil and milk and combine until it forms a dough (or mix in the food processor just enough for the dough to form a cohesive mass). Knead the dough a few turns, shape into a ball, coat with a few drops of olive oil, cover with an inverted bowl and let rest for at least 30 minutes or as long as overnight.

When ready to make the *torta*, divide the dough into a larger and smaller piece, shape each into a ball, rest for 15 minutes, then roll each piece into a larger and a smaller circle to fit the pan called for in your recipe. The larger circle should fit into the springform pan or pie plate with the edges overhanging by about 2 inches. Spoon the filling into the crust, top with the smaller circle of dough, fold the edges over the top of the *torta*, brush with beaten egg. Prick with a fork and bake in a preheated oven according to the recipe. (See filling recipes on pages 23, 24, 25.)

POTATO PIE
Torta di Patate

8 servings

- 1 recipe dough for *torte* (page 22)
- 2 pounds baking potatoes
- 2 tablespoons butter
- 2 tablespoons extra virgin olive oil
- 2 leeks, washed well and thinly sliced
- ½ teaspoon salt
- ¼ teaspoon freshly ground pepper
- ¼ teaspoon freshly grated nutmeg
- 2 eggs
- ½ cup warm milk
- ½ cup (2 ounces) freshly grated Parmigiano-Reggiano cheese
- Glaze: 1 beaten egg

Preheat oven to 375 degrees. Line a 10-inch pie plate or springform pan with the larger circle of dough allowing about 2 inches of the dough to overhang the edge and set aside.

Boil the potatoes in their jackets, cool slightly, peel, rice, and set aside in a medium bowl.

Heat the butter and olive oil in a medium skillet. Add the leeks along with the salt, pepper, and nutmeg and cook until softened. Add the leeks to the potatoes together with the eggs, milk, and cheese.

Spoon the potato mixture into the dough-lined pan, top with the smaller circle of dough, fold the edge over the top crust, brush with egg, prick with the tines of a fork in a decorative pattern. Bake in the preheated 375-degree oven for 50 to 60 minutes, or until the top is lightly golden.

RICE PIE 1

Torta di Riso 1

8 servings

- 1 recipe dough for *torte* (page 22)
- 1½ cups arborio rice
- 4 ounces butter, divided
- 4 scallions, cleaned and sliced
- ¼ cup dried porcini mushrooms, soaked, cleaned, and sliced
- salt and pepper to taste
- 2 eggs
- ½ cup mascarpone cheese
- ½ cup (2 ounces) freshly grated Parmigiano-Reggiano cheese
- Glaze: 1 beaten egg

Line a 10-inch pie plate or springform pan with the larger circle of dough, allowing about 2 inches of the dough to overhang the edge, and set aside.

Steam or boil the rice for only 10 minutes and drain (do not overcook since it will be baked). Add 2 ounces butter, mix and set aside. Preheat oven to 375 degrees.

Heat the rest of the butter in a small skillet and cook the scallions until limp. Add the mushrooms and some salt and pepper to taste and stir-fry in their own juices for 2 to 3 minutes. Add to the rice and mix together with the eggs, mascarpone, and Parmigiano-Reggiano cheese.

Spoon the rice mixture into the dough-lined pan, cover the filling with the smaller circle of dough, fold the 2-inch edge over the top crust, brush with egg, and prick the top with the tines of a fork in a decorative pattern. Bake in the preheated 375-degree oven for 50 to 60 minutes, or until the top is lightly golden.

RICE PIE 2

Torta di Riso 2

8 servings

The filling for this equally delicious variation of rice pie was made by Angiolina Berni, the mother of our friend Laura, even after she and her family moved to London from her native Bardi, a beautiful town in the Appennini mountains. This handwritten recipe from her kitchen notebook was brought to the United States by her daughter Laura who now resides in New Hampshire.

- 1 recipe dough for torte (page 22)
- 1½ cups arborio rice
- 4 ounces butter
- ¾ cup (3 ounces) finely grated Parmigiano-Reggiano cheese
- 2 eggs
- ½ cup milk or heavy cream
- Grated zest of 1 lemon

Prepare the filling as in the recipe for rice pie on the opposite page and let stand while you prepare the dough. Proceed to assemble and bake the torta as in the opposite recipe.

SPINACH PIE
Erbazzone

8 to 10 servings

PASTA FROLLA
FLAKY DOUGH:

2½ cups all-purpose flour

½ teaspoon salt

¼ cup lard, shortening, or butter

1 egg

¼ to ½ cup cold water

SPINACH FILLING:

2 10-ounce bags fresh spinach or 2 10-ounce packages frozen spinach

salt and pepper to taste

1 cup (4 ounces) grated Parmigiano-Reggiano cheese

2 cups fresh ricotta cheese

2 eggs

Freshly grated nutmeg

Glaze: 1 beaten egg

Preheat oven to 375 degrees.

Prepare dough: By hand or in a food processor, mix the flour and salt, cut the fat into the flour, and add the egg and enough water to make a soft dough. Knead a few turns without overworking the dough. Wrap in plastic and refrigerate while preparing the filling.

Prepare filling: If using fresh spinach, wash the spinach with great care to remove all traces of grit. Drop into boiling water for 2 minutes, strain, and squeeze dry. If using frozen spinach, defrost and squeeze dry. Add to the spinach some salt and pepper, the grated Parmigiano-Reggiano, ricotta, and eggs, and set aside.

Roll the dough with a pasta machine or by hand. If rolling it out by hand, divide the dough into thirds and use two-thirds for the bottom crust and one-third for the top. Place the larger one in a lightly oiled or sprayed 10-inch springform pan, allowing the dough to overhang the rim of the pan by 2 inches.

Spoon the filling into the dough-lined pan, cover with the second disk, fold the overhanging dough over the top crust and brush with beaten egg. Prick the top in a decorative pattern.

Bake in the preheated 375-degree oven for 50 to 60 minutes or until the top crust begins to color. Cool on a rack for 30 minutes or more before serving either hot or at room temperature. Unmold and serve.

HAM AND CHEESE PIE

Torta di Prosciutto Cotto e Fontina

8 servings

1 recipe flaky dough (page 26)
8 ounces cooked ham, sliced
8 ounces Italian Fontina cheese, sliced
Glaze: 1 beaten egg

Preheat oven to 375 degrees.

Divide the pastry in half, and roll out each piece into a 12-inch circle. Place one circle on a baking sheet. Arrange the ham slices on top of the dough to about 1 inch from the edge. Top with slices of fontina cheese.

Brush the edge of the dough circle with beaten egg and cover with the second circle of dough. Press the top and the bottom edges together with the tines of a fork. Brush the top with beaten egg, prick with a fork in a decorative pattern. Bake in the preheated 375 degree oven for 45 minutes or until lightly golden.

CHESTNUT FRITTERS

Frittelle di Castagne

6 to 8 servings

This recipe was made for Gianni and Giorgio Grassi by their aunt Irene Franceschini in the beautiful hill town of Berceto while they stayed with her as children during WWII. I thank Dr. Giorgio Grassi for the recipe.

- 1½ cups chestnut flour
- pinch of salt
- 3 tablespoons sugar
- 3 tablespoons extra virgin olive oil
- 1 cup cold water
- ½ cup vegetable oil
- 1 cup fresh ricotta cheese

Mix the chestnut flour, salt, sugar, and olive oil. Add the water and mix well with a wooden spoon. Let stand for at least one hour.

Heat the vegetable oil in a skillet. Drop the batter into the hot oil by tablespoonfuls, flattening slightly. Let brown on one side, turn and brown the other side. Drain on paper towels.

Top each fritter with a teaspoonful of ricotta and serve hot or at room temperature.

ROASTED CHESTNUTS
CASTAGNE ARROSTITE

Majestic chestnut trees dot the landscape of Emilia-Romagna. Chestnuts have historically been a guarantee against the lean years and were once considered the food of the poor because they are plentiful, easily available, sweet, and very nutritious. Of course, they are enjoyed by everybody as a traditional food that is as versatile as it is delicious.

Fragrant, freshly roasted chestnuts are still a favorite snack or an after-dinner treat. To make them take 1 pound of chestnuts and cut an X on each chestnut with the point of a paring knife. Bake in a preheated 400 degree oven for 20 minutes. Or place in a chestnut roaster (a frying pan with large holes all over the bottom), and gently shake the pan on top of the stove as the chestnuts roast and release their fragrance. Whether baked or roasted, wrap in a towel and let rest for 15 minutes before shelling them while still hot, removing the inner skin. Enjoy the roasted chestnuts with a glass of Lambrusco.

FRESH NOODLES AND FILLED PASTA

Pasta Fresca e Tortelli

PASTA FRESCA E TORTELLI
FRESH NOODLES AND FILLED PASTA

Prosciutto and Melon (Prosciutto e Melone), page 8

Prosciutto and Asparagus (Prosciutto e Asparagi), page 9

Hand-shaped Ridged Tubular Pasta (Garganelli), page 40

Lasagne Bolognese (Lasagne alla Bolognese), page 46

Ricotta and Spinach Dumplings (Malfatti), page 47

Stuffed Noodle Roll (Rotolo di Pasta), page 53

Polenta with Wild Mushroom Stew (Polenta con Spezzatino di Funghi), page 88

Sausage with Lentils (Cotechino con Lenticchie), page 101

Ossobuco Romagna-style (Ossobuco alla Romagnola), page 107

Fried Trout (Trota Fritta), page 112

Fresh Noodle Tart from Ferrara (Torta Ferrarese), page 146

Plum Tart (Crostata di Susine), page 150

Stuffed Baked Peaches (Pesche Ripiene al Forno), page 161

EGG NOODLES
Tagliatelle

Tagliatelle *really define the cooking of Emilia-Romagna.* Sfoglie *or freshly rolled out sheets of egg noodles, green or white, cut into* tagliatelle *(noodles), hand shaped into* Garganelli *and* Stricchetti, *filled to make* tortelli *(filled pasta) to serve with sauce and tortellini (small filled pasta for soup) to add to meat broths are the triumphs of the cooking of Emilia-Romagna. The women who traditionally dedicated themselves to making fresh pasta with skilled hands at lightning speed are called "*sfogline*" a term which comes from the word for the thinly rolled out sheet of dough, "*sfoglia.*" Many restaurants in Emilia-Romagna pride themselves in still having* sfogline *on their staff to prepare this artisanal specialty.*

3 cups all-purpose flour
4 large eggs

Freshly made tagliatelle

Using your hands or a food processor, mix the flour and eggs into a rather stiff dough. Add water or additional flour 1 tablespoon at a time until the dough comes together in a ball but is not sticky. Knead a few turns by hand until smooth, shape into a ball, coat with a few drops of olive oil, cover with a bowl and let rest for 30 minutes.

Roll out the dough by hand using a rolling pin, sprinkling the sheet of dough liberally with flour and turning it to get an even thickness through which you can see your hand (or use a pasta machine). Coat the sheet of dough with flour, roll loosely into a tube, and cut into ¼-inch or ½-inch strips unfolding the strips as you cut them. Place the noodles on a towel-lined pan, sprinkle with flour and gently toss it with your hands to separate the strands. Cook according to recipe instructions or in salted boiling water until just al dente.

SPINACH NOODLES
Tagliatelle Verdi

3½ cups all-purpose flour
4 large eggs
5 ounces fresh spinach, blanched, drained, squeezed dry, and finely chopped; *or* 1 10-ounce package frozen chopped spinach, cooked, cooled, and squeezed dry

Mix the dough as for the plain *tagliatelle* recipe (page 35) except add the spinach. Knead and roll out the dough as for the plain *tagliatelle*.

NOODLES HAND CUT IN IRREGULAR SHAPES
Maltagliati

Maltagliati *are particularly delicious in bean soup or minestrone.*

Cut the sheet of *tagliatelle* dough (page 35) into 1-inch strips. Lay the lightly floured strips one on top of the other on your cutting board and cut them crosswise into irregular triangular shapes. Place in a towel-lined pan and gently toss them with your hands to separate the pieces, sprinkling a little additional flour if necessary.

Cook according to your recipe's instructions or in salted boiling water until just al dente.

SMALL HAND-CHOPPED PASTA FOR SOUP

Malfattini

This pasta is cooked in meat broth and served with the traditional* nevicata *which means an abundant "snowfall" of freshly grated Parmigiano-Reggiano cheese.

After you make the *tagliatelle* dough (page 35), shape it into a ball but do not coat with oil or cover—leave on your board to air dry for 30 to 45 minutes.

Cut the dough into rather thick slices and let dry again. Cut the slices into pieces and chop with either a *mezza-luna*, the traditional Italian half-moon-shaped chopping knife, or with a chef's knife until you have granules the size of rice kernels. Place in a towel-lined pan, sprinkle with flour, and gently toss with your hands to separate the pieces.

Cook according to your recipe's instructions or serve as described above.

FINE EGG NOODLES

Taglierini

These noodles are delicious added to beef or chicken broth, and excellent for use in* torta Ferrarese *(page 146) and* bassotti *(page 45).

Roll out the sheet of *tagliatelle* dough (page 35) paper thin and cut the noodles as fine as possible.

Cook according to your recipe's instructions or serve as described above.

TINY BREAD DUMPLINGS FOR SOUP

Passatelli

4 to 6 servings

Growing up in Italy, when my cousin Vana Muccio, a native of Ferrara, made passatelli *it was always a treat for myself and her children, Luisella and Gianfranco. These are a fast, easy, and delicious addition to a good broth for a delicious soup. Make the* passatelli *while the broth is coming to a boil, then drop them directly into the boiling liquid and stir gently to separate.*

- ¾ cup fresh breadcrumbs
- ¾ cup (3 ounces) freshly grated Parmigiano-Reggiano cheese, plus additional for serving
- 1 ounce beef marrow or butter, room temperature
- 3 large eggs
- pinch of nutmeg

Mix all ingredients to make a dough.

Push the dough through the holes of the traditional tool used in Emilia-Romagna for this purpose or use a potato masher or food mill, inserting the disk with the largest holes.

Add the pasta to boiling meat broth. The *passatelli* are done when they all float to the surface.

Shaping the passatelli *with the traditional tool ...*

and passatelli *ready to be dropped into boiling broth*

HAND-SHAPED RIDGED TUBULAR AND BUTTERFLY PASTA

Garganelli and Stricchetti

Garganelli ***and*** **stricchetti** ***are made with an egg dough further enriched by a touch of freshly grated Parmigiano-Reggiano cheese. Historically cooked in broth and served as a soup, their size is now considered more appropriate to serve as*** **pasta asciutta** ***or strained pasta with sauce. Both are fun to make with the help of family and friends including children.***

3 cups all-purpose flour
4 eggs
1 cup (4 ounces) grated Parmigiano Reggiano cheese
pinch of salt
pinch of nutmeg

Using either your hands or a food processor mix the dough ingredients until a solid smooth ball forms that is not too sticky. Use to make *garganelli* or *stricchetti* as instructed below.

Garganelli
Hand-Shaped Ridged Tubular Pasta

Buy a set of wooden paddles with ridges, those that were traditionally used to make decorative butter balls but that are now marketed as gnocchi makers. Have a dowel the thickness of a pencil cut into 6-inch lengths. Roll out the dough evenly and thinly and cut into 1½-inch squares with a fluted pastry wheel. Take a square of dough and starting with one corner roll it around the dowel. Then, holding the two ends of the dowel, press and roll the dough on the paddle to make ridges on the piece of pasta. Slide the pasta off the dowel onto a towel-lined pan to dry until ready to cook. Continue until all the dough is used.

Stricchetti
Butterfly Pasta

Roll out the dough either by hand or with a noodle machine. Using a fluted pastry wheel cut 2-inch squares, pinch the middle of each piece tightly to make a butterfly or bow-tie shape. Place them on floured kitchen towels until you're ready to cook and serve them with your favorite sauce.

Egg dough cut into squares with a pastry wheel for garganelli *...*

wrapping the dough on the dowel and shaping the garganelli *on the ridged board ...*

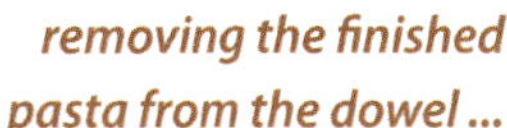

removing the finished pasta from the dowel ...

and the fresh garganelli *drying until ready to cook*

GARGANELLI IN THE STYLE OF LUGO
GARGANELLI DI LUGO

Lugo claims to be the birthplace of *garganelli* and serves them with a variety of sauces. The town, which is just west of the medieval city of Ravenna, boasts a Town Hall housed in a 14th-century castle, an arcaded market place, and a cooking school where you can learn to make *garganelli* and other specialties of the region under the direction of Chef Nadia Montuschi. In Lugo, this traditional pasta is served *asciutta*, meaning drained, with a variety of sauces and vegetables, rather than cooked in broth as was the original custom.

GARGANELLI "GYPSY-STYLE"
Garganelli alla "Zingara"

6 to 8 servings

This typical local recipe was submitted by Chef Nadia Montuschi from the Ala d'Oro Hotel in Lugo.

4 ounces pancetta, chopped
1 onion, sliced
2 red or green bell peppers, sliced
8 ounces fresh mushrooms, sliced
2 ripe tomatoes, peeled and chopped
salt to taste
pinch of red pepper flakes
one recipe *garganelli* pasta (page 40)

Place the pancetta, onion, and peppers in a sauté pan and cook until pancetta is crisp and the vegetables softened. Add the mushrooms and cook for five minutes. Add the tomatoes, salt and pepper to taste, and the red pepper flakes and cook for 15 more minutes.

Cook the *garganelli* in salted water until just al dente. Drain. Add the cooked *garganelli* to the sauce and gently toss for 2 minutes.

MEAT SAUCE FROM LUGO

Ragù Romagnolo di Lugo

6 to 8 servings

This is one of the sauces served in Lugo over garganelli.

- 1 ounce dried porcini mushrooms
- *battuto*: 2 ounces prosciutto, 1 carrot, 1 onion, and 1 celery rib
- 2 ounces butter
- 1 pound ground pork or beef, or a combination of the two
- 6 ounces tomato paste
- 1 cup Sangiovese wine
- 2 cups beef or chicken broth
- salt and pepper to taste
- pinch of nutmeg
- 1 10-ounce package frozen peas, defrosted

Soak the dried mushrooms in 1 cup of warm water for 30 minutes. Drain, reserving the soaking water, rinse well, chop, and set aside.

Meanwhile make the *battuto* by finely chopping together the prosciutto, carrot, onion, and celery with either a *mezzaluna*, the traditional Italian "half moon" chopper, or a chef's knife. Set aside.

Heat the butter in a saucepan, add the *battuto* and the mushrooms and stir-fry until the vegetables dry out and become fragrant. Add the meat and stir to separate and brown. Make a hot spot by moving the meat to the sides of the pan with your wooden spoon, add the tomato paste and cook for a minute or two while stirring. Add the wine, stir with all the ingredients and let it reduce for 15 minutes as it flavors the mixture.

Add the broth, bring to a boil, add salt and pepper to taste and a fresh grinding of nutmeg. Lower the heat to the barest simmer, cover and cook for 1¼ hours, stirring from time to time and adding the reserved mushroom soaking water in small quantities.

Add the defrosted peas and any of the mushroom water left, and cook for another 15 minutes. Serve over *garganelli* (page 40) cooked al dente.

CHESTNUT FLOUR NOODLES WITH RICOTTA SAUCE

Tagliatelle di Castagne con Salsa di Ricotta

4 to 6 servings

Most recipes for these noodles call for a mixture of chestnut and all-purpose flour, but my friend Annamaria Clerici, who is a fabulous and very knowledgeable home cook, taught me a special technique to make her delicious full-bodied and very flavorful chestnut noodles. I made Tagliatelle di Castagne *many times for our Aunt Elvira and each time she felt transported to her beloved town of Berceto.*

CHESTNUT FLOUR NOODLES:

2 cups chestnut flour

1 cup boiling water

All-purpose flour to roll out the noodles

RICOTTA SAUCE:

2 cups fresh ricotta cheese

½ cup milk

Optional topping: ¼ cup walnuts, coarsely chopped

NOTE: Although the chestnut noodles can be hand mixed, they are best made in a food processor.

Add the boiling water to the chestnut flour all at once and mix quickly into a dense and smooth dough. Shape into a ball and let stand for 30 minutes.

Divide the dough in half, sprinkle with flour so that it doesn't stick to the board, and roll out into a thin sheet. Since this is a delicate dough, keep it flat on the board and cut the sheet into broad strips making sure that the sheet is well-coated with flour. Let the noodles dry until ready to cook and serve.

Place the ricotta in a serving bowl and mix with the milk until smooth. Meanwhile, bring a pot of water to a boil, salt to taste, add the chestnut noodles and cook until they come to the surface. Lift the noodles out of the water with a skimmer and place in the bowl on top of the ricotta sauce. Gently toss to coat and top with the walnuts, if using.

BAKED NOODLES
Bassotti

6 to 8 servings

Bassotti ***are one of a class of recipes unique to Emilia-Romagna in which very fine, uncooked, freshly made egg noodles are layered with other seasonings and baked.*** **Bassotti** ***are savory whereas*** **Torta Ferrarese** ***and*** **Torta di Modena** ***are the sweet versions.***

- ¼ cup breadcrumbs
- 1 recipe *taglierini* (page 37)
- 1 stick butter
- 1 cup (4 ounces) freshly grated Parmigiano-Reggiano cheese
- 1 cup chicken broth

Preheat oven to 350 degrees.

Butter a round or square pyrex baking dish, cover the bottom with breadcrumbs, place a layer of freshly made uncooked noodles on top of the breadcrumbs. Dot the noodles with ⅓ of the butter and sprinkle with ⅓ of the Parmigiano-Reggiano. Repeat the layers twice more. Carefully pour the broth down the side of the dish. Place the baking dish in a larger pan to catch any possible drippings.

Bake in the preheated 350-degree oven for 30 to 40 minutes or until the top is crisp and golden and the liquid has been absorbed.

LASAGNE BOLOGNESE

Lasagne alla Bolognese

6 to 8 servings

So typical of Bologna is this dish that you can even buy it at the railroad station, and it's delicious even there, attesting to the pride that Bologna takes in its cuisine.

- Dough from 1 recipe *tagliatelle verdi* (page 36)
- 3 cups classic Bolognese sauce plus 1 cup to pass around at the table (page 124)
- 3 cups béchamel sauce (page 123)
- 2 cups (8 ounces) freshly grated Parmigiano-Reggiano cheese
- 2 ounces butter

Roll out the dough into lasagne noodles 4 or 5 inches wide and about 5 or 6 inches long (or as long as the pan). Place them on a floured towel until you are ready to boil them.

Bring a large pot of water to a boil, put in 4 or 5 lasagne noodles, boil them for 2 minutes or until they come to the surface, take out with a skimmer, dunk in cold water, and place them on a clean towel. Continue until all the noodles are cooked.

Preheat oven to 375 degrees. Spoon 2 tablespoons of Bolognese sauce on the bottom of a 9-by-12-inch pyrex baking pan, place a layer of lasagne noodles on top, spoon and spread 2 to 3 tablespoons of Bolognese sauce on top of the lasagne noodles, distribute 2 to 3 tablespoons of béchamel sauce over, and complete with 2 tablespoons of grated Parmigiano-Reggiano. Continue to layer the ingredients until the pan is full. (*Lasagne al forno* can have as few as 3 layers and as many as 8.) The final layer can be just some béchamel sauce and Parmigiano-Reggiano dotted with the butter or you can also add some of the Bolognese sauce.

Bake the lasagne in the preheated 375-degree oven for 30 to 40 minutes or until the top has formed a thin crust and the contents are bubbly (you will need to adjust the time depending on the number of layers). Let the lasagne set for 30 minutes before cutting and serving. Cut the lasagne in half or in thirds lengthwise and then into 6 or 8 portions.

RICOTTA AND SPINACH DUMPLINGS
Malfatti

6 to 8 servings

Cleonige, the cook of the Musa family, made these for us on our honeymoon visit to Bedonia and they have remained one of our very favorite treats.

- 2 cups fresh dry ricotta cheese (*see note*)
- 2 10-ounce bags fresh spinach, blanched, drained, squeezed dry, and chopped; *or* 2 10-ounce packages frozen chopped spinach, cooked, cooled, and squeezed dry
- 1 cup (4 ounces) freshly grated Parmigiano-Reggiano cheese plus ½ cup for topping
- 1 egg
- pinch of nutmeg
- 1 cup all-purpose flour
- 1 stick (4 ounces) butter, melted

Mix the ricotta, spinach, 1 cup of Parmigiano-Reggiano, egg, and nutmeg. Shape into walnut-size balls. Roll each ball in flour, place in a towel-lined pan and let rest in a cool place or in the refrigerator until ready to cook.

Fill a wide shallow pan halfway with water and bring to a boil. Drop the *malfatti* one at a time into the boiling water. The *malfatti* are cooked when they come to the surface and float. Lift them out of the water with a skimmer and place directly into individual serving dishes with 6 to 8 *malfatti* per portion. Drizzle with melted butter and top with grated Parmigiano-Reggiano cheese. (Leftovers can be placed in a casserole, drizzled with butter, topped with Parmigiano-Reggiano and heated through in the oven.)

NOTE: *Malfatti* are made from the filling of *tortelli* and require a rather dry ricotta cheese available in Italian markets and sold in aluminum containers with pin holes on the side which allow it to drain. If using commercial ricotta, place it in a cheesecloth-lined colander and allow to drain overnight in the refrigerator before measuring the needed amount.

SPINACH-FILLED PASTA

Tortelli di Spinaci

6 to 8 servings

Tortelli ***are a class of filled pasta that enclose a variety of vegetable, meat, or cheese fillings in fresh square or rectangular egg noodle pockets. They are served with melted butter or sauce and a*** **nevicata di Parmigiano-Reggiano** ***(a "snowfall" of freshly grated Parmigiano-Reggiano).***

NOTE: This filling requires a rather dry ricotta cheese available in Italian markets and sold in aluminum containers with pin holes on the side which allow it to drain. If using commercial ricotta, place it in a cheesecloth-lined colander and allow to drain overnight in the refrigerator before measuring the needed amount.

1 recipe *tagliatelle* dough (page 35)

SPINACH FILLING:

2 cups fresh dry ricotta (*see note*)

2 10-ounce bags fresh spinach, blanched, drained, squeezed dry, and chopped; *or* 2 10-ounce packages frozen chopped spinach, cooked, cooled, and squeezed dry

1 cup (4 ounces) freshly grated Parmigiano-Reggiano cheese plus ½ cup for topping

1 egg

pinch of nutmeg

Mix the filling ingredients in a large bowl and set aside.

Roll out the dough thinly into a 12-by-6-inch rectangular sheet with a rolling pin or with a pasta machine set to one setting before the last.

Place 1-tablespoon mounds of filling on the long side of each dough sheet about 2 inches from the edge and 2 inches apart. Fold the dough on top of the filling, lightly press with your fingertips around the filling to be sure that the top and bottom sheets of dough adhere to each other and that air bubbles are expelled. Cut around the mounds of filling on three sides with a scalloped pastry wheel to make 2-inch-square *tortellis*. Make sure that the edges are well adhered. Place on a towel-lined tray until ready to cook.

Bring a large pot of water to a boil. Drop the *tortelli* one by one into the boiling water, let them come to the surface, cook 2 minutes, lift out of the cooking water with a skimmer and place into a serving platter. Serve topped with melted butter and freshly grated Parmigiano-Reggiano, or with Bolognese sauce (pages 125 or 126) and freshly grated Parmigiano-Reggiano.

CHESTNUT-FILLED PASTA
Tortelli di Castagne

6 to 8 servings

1 recipe *tagliatelle* dough (page 35)

CHESTNUT FILLING:

1 pound fresh chestnuts; *or* 1 10-ounce jar ready-to-use prepared chestnuts

1 cup ricotta cheese

½ cup (2 ounces) freshly grated Parmigiano-Reggiano cheese

salt, pepper, and freshly grated nutmeg to taste

TOPPING:

4 ounces (2 tablespoons) melted butter

¼ cup freshly grated Parmigiano-Reggiano cheese

Boil the fresh chestnuts, if using, and peel while hot and remove the inner skin.

Place the chestnuts in a food processor and puree or rice as you would potatoes. Add the ricotta, Parmigiano-Reggiano, salt, pepper, and nutmeg, and mix. Set aside.

Roll out the dough thinly into a 12-by-6-inch rectangular sheet with a rolling pin or with a pasta machine set to one setting before the last.

Place 1-tablespoon mounds of filling on the long side of each dough sheet about 2 inches from the edge and 2 inches apart. Fold the dough on top of the filling, lightly press with your fingertips around the filling to be sure that the top and bottom sheets of dough adhere to each other and that air bubbles are expelled. Cut around the mounds of filling on three sides with a scalloped pastry wheel to make 2-inch-square *tortellis*. Make sure that the edges are well adhered. Place on a towel-lined tray until ready to cook.

Bring a large pot of water to a boil. Drop the *tortelli* one by one into the boiling water, let them come to the surface, cook 2 minutes, lift out of the cooking water with a skimmer and place into a serving platter. Serve topped with melted butter and freshly grated Parmigiano-Reggiano, or with Bolognese sauce (pages 125 or 126) and freshly grated Parmigiano-Reggiano.

DRIED CHESTNUT-FILLED PASTA

Tortelli di Castagne Secche

6 to 8 servings

Dried chestnuts are available all year and are easier to prepare than their fresh cousins. This recipe is entirely different from the previous one although either one can be made with fresh or dried chestnuts.

- 1 recipe *tagliatelle* dough (page 35)
- 8 ounces dried chestnuts, soaked overnight
- 4 ounces finely chopped *mostarda* (Italian preserved fruits)

Boil the soaked chestnuts in their soaking water until soft, 1 to 1½ hours. Drain, reserving water, and process chestnuts into a puree.

Place the chestnut puree into a bowl, fold in the chopped *mostarda* fruit, and enough of the chestnut cooking water to soften the mixture if it is too stiff. Set aside the filling.

Roll out the dough thinly into a 12-by-6-inch rectangular sheet with a rolling pin or with a pasta machine set to one setting before the last.

Place 1-tablespoon mounds of filling on the long side of each dough sheet about 2 inches from the edge and 2 inches apart. Fold the dough on top of the filling, lightly press with your fingertips around the filling to be sure that the top and bottom sheets of dough adhere to each other and that air bubbles are expelled. Cut around the mounds of filling on three sides with a scalloped pastry wheel to make 2-inch-square *tortellis*. Make sure that the edges are well adhered. Place on a towel-lined tray until ready to cook.

Bring a large pot of water to a boil. Drop the *tortelli* one by one into the boiling water, let them come to the surface, cook 2 minutes, lift out of the cooking water with a skimmer and place into a serving platter. Serve topped with melted butter and freshly grated Parmigiano-Reggiano, or with Bolognese sauce (pages 125 or 126) and freshly grated Parmigiano-Reggiano.

SQUASH-FILLED PASTA

Tortelli di Zucca

6 to 8 servings

1 recipe *tagliatelle* dough (page 35)

SQUASH FILLING:

1 butternut squash

8 Amaretti di Saronno cookies, processed into crumbs

1 cup (4 ounces) freshly grated Parmigiano-Reggiano cheese

pinch of freshly grated nutmeg

pinch of salt

optional: 1 tablespoon finely chopped *mostarda* (Italian preserved fruits)

Cut the squash in half, prick the skin with a fork, place cut side down on a baking sheet and bake in a 375-degree oven for 40 to 50 minutes or until soft. Remove the seeds, spoon the pulp out of its skin and put through a food mill. Drain in a fine colander to remove excess liquid.

Mix the squash pulp with the amaretti crumbs, Parmigiano-Reggiano, nutmeg, salt, and *mostarda*, if using. Set the filling aside.

Roll out the dough thinly into a 12-by-6-inch rectangular sheet with a rolling pin or with a pasta machine set to one setting before the last.

Place 1-tablespoon mounds of filling on the long side of each dough sheet about 2 inches from the edge and 2 inches apart. Fold the dough on top of the filling, lightly press with your fingertips around the filling to be sure that the top and bottom sheets of dough adhere to each other and that air bubbles are expelled. Cut around the mounds of filling on three sides with a scalloped pastry wheel to make 2-inch-square *tortellis*. Make sure that the edges are well adhered. Place on a towel-lined tray until ready to cook.

Bring a large pot of water to a boil. Drop the *tortelli* one by one into the boiling water, let them come to the surface, cook 2 minutes, lift out of the cooking water with a skimmer and place into a serving platter. Serve topped with melted butter and freshly grated Parmigiano-Reggiano, or with Bolognese sauce (pages 125 or 126) and freshly grated Parmigiano-Reggiano.

STUFFED NOODLE ROLL

Rotolo di Pasta

6 to 8 servings

½ recipe *tagliatelle* dough (page 35)

FILLING:

2 cups fresh ricotta cheese, drained overnight

2 10-ounce bags fresh spinach, blanched, drained, squeezed dry and chopped; *or* 2 10-ounce packages frozen chopped spinach, cooked, cooled, and squeezed dry

1 cup (4 ounces) freshly grated Parmigiano-Reggiano cheese

1 egg

pinch of nutmeg

TOPPINGS:

1 stick (4 ounces) butter, melted

½ cup (2 ounces) freshly grated Parmigiano-Reggiano cheese

Roll the pasta dough into a 12-by-14-inch rectangle. Mix all the filling ingredients together. Spread the filling on the dough and roll up from the longer side like a jelly roll. Place the roll on a piece of cheesecloth, wrap it and tie the two ends with kitchen twine.

Fill a fish poacher half full with water, bring to a boil and add 1 tablespoon of salt. Carefully lower the noodle roll into the water, cover, bring the water back to a boil, lower the heat and simmer for 30 minutes.

Lift the noodle roll out of the pan, let cool until you can handle it. Untie the ends, remove the cheesecloth, cut into 1-inch slices and place on a serving platter in a single layer. Drizzle with melted butter and top with freshly grated Parmigiano-Reggiano cheese.

RAVIOLO WITH EGG YOLK

Raviolo con L'uovo

4 servings

It is said that one should have this sensational dish at least once for a truly memorable gourmet experience. It is a large, single serving raviolo *filled with herbed ricotta with an egg yolk cradled in the middle which spills out like sunshine when you cut into it. This was the signature dish of the famous New York restaurant San Domenico (the counterpart of the equally famous restaurant by the same name near Bologna in the town of Imola), which had happily reopened as SD 26 on 26th Street and Madison Avenue in New York City, still had the raviolo on the menu before it closed permanently.*

4 10-by-5-inch strips of rolled out *tagliatelle* dough (page 35)

4 egg yolks

BASIC FILLING:

1½ cups fresh ricotta cheese, drained overnight before measuring

½ cup freshly grated Parmigiano-Reggiano cheese (2 ounces)

pinch of freshly grated nutmeg

pinch of salt

½ teaspoon fresh marjoram, chopped; *or* 1 teaspoon Italian flat-leaf parsley, finely chopped; *or* ½ teaspoon grated lemon zest

Mix all the filling ingredients in a medium bowl and set aside.

Place 2 strips of dough on your counter. Place the filling in two mounds about 2½ inches from the ends and 5 inches apart on each of the two strips. Using the back of a spoon, make depressions in the ricotta filling and carefully fill each with an egg yolk being careful not to break them.

Lightly moisten the dough around the filling with water, place the other two strips of dough on top of the filling. Carefully press the top and bottom sheet of dough around the filling to adhere and to remove any air bubbles. Center a fluted 4-inch cutter on each *raviolo* and cut into a circle. (If you don't have a cutter, center a bowl around each *raviolo* and using it as a guide, cut each with a scalloped ravioli cutting wheel.) Carefully place the *raviolo* on a floured towel until ready to cook.

TOPPINGS:

Thinly sliced fresh truffles (if you can permit yourself such a luxury); *or* 1 tablespoon truffle oil

4 ounces butter, melted and cooked until fragrant and beginning to brown

Freshly grated Parmigiano-Reggiano cheese

When ready to serve, bring a wide, low pot of water to a boil and add some salt to taste. Add the *raviolo* one at a time and cook for 2 minutes. Remove from the water with a skimmer and place directly in each serving plate. Mix the truffles or truffle oil with the brown butter and then drizzle on the *raviolo* and shower with freshly grated Parmigiano-Reggiano.

MEAT-FILLED PASTA
Tortellini di Carne

6 to 8 servings

1 recipe *tagliatelle* dough (page 35)

MEAT FILLING:

2 tablespoons butter

8 ounces boneless pork loin, sliced

4 ounces prosciutto, chopped

4 ounces mortadella, chopped

½ cup (2 ounces) freshly grated Parmigiano-Reggiano cheese

fresh grinding of nutmeg

1 egg yolk

1 egg white, as needed

Melt the butter in a small frying pan, add the pork and stir until it begins to color. Cover the pan, lower the heat and cook for 10 more minutes in the pan juices; if it gets too dry add 1 tablespoon of broth or water. Cool in the pan, then, with a rubber spatula pour the contents of the pan into a food processor. Add the prosciutto and mortadella and process until combined and pureed. Spoon into a bowl and fold in the Parmigiano-Reggiano, nutmeg, egg yolk and enough egg white to just make a thick paste.

Roll out the dough thinly by hand or with a pasta machine. Using a sharp knife or a plain pastry wheel, cut the dough into 1¼-inch squares. Cover the dough with a towel to keep it from drying. Working in batches so that the dough doesn't dry out, place a small mound of filling (the size of a marble) in the middle of each square of dough, fold to form a triangle, pinch the edges to be sure that they are closed, then turn the two closed sides of the triangle around your index finger with the apex of the triangle facing up and pinch tightly together so that the individual tortellini don't come apart. If necessary dab the edges with a little water to be sure that they are sealed. As the tortellini are made place in a towel-covered pan until ready to cook. If they are not going to be cooked in 1 to 2 hours they should be refrigerated or frozen. (Cut any leftover dough into *maltagliati*, and air dry, to add to soup.)

Bring a large pot of water to a boil, add some salt and gently add the *tortellini* and cook until they all float to the top. Gently remove from the water with a skimmer. Serve with your favorite topping.

CHEESE-FILLED PASTA
Tortellini di Magro

6 to 8 servings

1 recipe *tagliatelle* dough (page 35)

CHEESE FILLING:

1½ cups fresh ricotta cheese, drained overnight and then measured

4 ounces *stracchino* cheese or American cream cheese

1 cup (4 ounces) freshly grated Parmigiano-Reggiano cheese

fresh grinding of nutmeg

salt to taste

1 egg yolk

1 egg white, as needed

Mix all the filling ingredients except the egg white in a food processor. Add just enough egg white to make a thick paste.

Roll out the dough thinly by hand or with a pasta machine. Using a sharp knife or a plain pastry wheel, cut the dough into 1¼-inch squares. Cover the dough with a towel to keep it from drying. Working in batches so that the dough doesn't dry out, place a small mound of filling (the size of a marble) in the middle of each square of dough, fold to form a triangle, pinch the edges to be sure that they are closed, then turn the two sides of the triangle around your index finger with the apex of the triangle facing up and pinch together tightly so that the *tortellini* don't come apart. If necessary dab the edges with a little water to be sure that they are sealed. As the *tortellini* are made place in a towel-covered pan until ready to cook. If they are not going to be cooked in 1 to 2 hours they should be refrigerated or frozen.

Bring a large pot of water to a boil, add some salt and gently add the *tortellini* and cook until they all float to the top. Gently remove from the water with a skimmer. Serve with your favorite topping.

STUFFED PASTA IN BROTH

Anolini di Parma

6 to 8 servings

Anolini *are the quintessential stuffed pasta of Parma. They are made from the pan juices of the* stracotto di Parma *(page 103), a slow-cooked pot roast. My friend Isabella Musa cooks her* stracotto *for 24 hours as she remembers her mother doing. Today, most Parmigiani give it a briefer cooking while still extracting all possible flavor from their pot roast. Some cooks add ¼ cup of the finely chopped* stracotto *beef to the* anolini *filling, but traditionally it's made with only* la bagna*—the dense and full-flavored pan juices of the* stracotto.

8 cups capon or chicken broth

½ cup or more freshly grated Parmigiano-Reggiano cheese

FILLING:

¾ cup dry breadcrumbs

1 cup (4 ounces) freshly grated Parmigiano-Reggiano cheese

freshly grated nutmeg

¾ cup *stracotto* sauce (page 103)

1 egg, beaten

ANOLINI DOUGH:

2 cups all-purpose flour

2 eggs plus 1 beaten egg for brushing

2 egg yolks

pinch of salt

For the filling, mix the breadcrumbs, Parmigiano-Reggiano cheese, a pinch of nutmeg, and the cold *stracotto* sauce with as much egg as necessary to make a thick paste. Mix well and refrigerate overnight.

Mix all the dough ingredients by hand or in a food processor. Knead a few turns by hand, shape into a ball, brush with a few drops of olive oil, cover with an inverted bowl, and let rest for 30 minutes.

Divide the dough into 4 pieces and roll each portion very thinly into a circle by hand or into a long strip by machine. Lightly brush one sheet of dough with some of the beaten egg, spoon small mounds of filling in rows about 1½ inches apart. Cover with another sheet of dough, press around each mound to be sure that the two pieces of dough are well adhered, and cut the *anolini* using the traditional *Bosso* or wooden boxwood cutter, or a ¾-inch round cutter. (*Anolini* are round in Parma and half moons in Piacenza.) Place the finished *anolini* on a floured cotton towel until you are ready to drop them in boiling broth. Make additional *anolini* with the other two sheets. (Scraps of dough can be gathered, pressed together, and rolled to make more *anolini*, or they can be made into *maltagliati*, that is, allowed to dry slightly before cutting them coarsely into uneven shapes to add to soups.)

To cook the *anolini*: Measure the number of *anolini* per person by placing enough *anolini* in a soup plate to cover the bottom in a single layer. That will be one portion. Bring the broth to a boil, add the *anolini*, and cook until all have come to the surface. Taste one to be sure that it's done to your desired tenderness. Serve each portion with some broth and top with grated Parmigiano-Reggiano cheese.

Anolini di Parma *filling is spaced on a piece of egg dough ...*

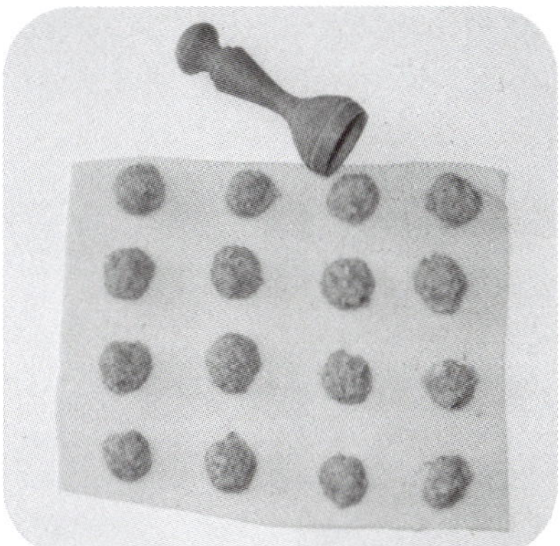

then covered with another sheet of dough ...

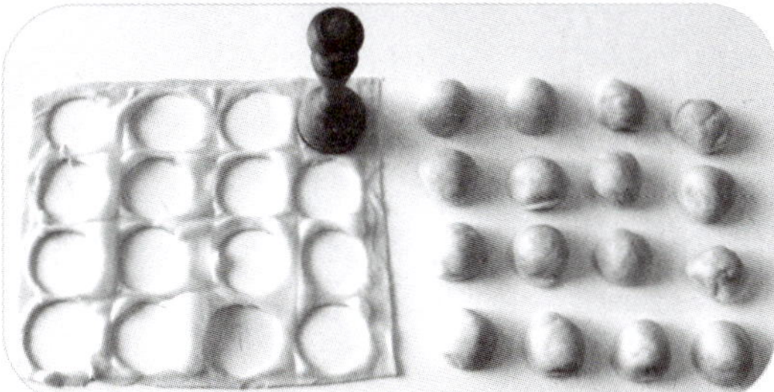

cut with the traditional wooden tool and removed ...

and cooked and served in a delicious broth

BROTHS AND SOUPS

Brodi e Minestre

BRODI E MINESTRE
BROTHS AND SOUPS

MEAT BROTH
Brodo di Carne

Makes about 2 quarts

If the broth is the main event, start with cold water. If the meat is to take center stage, start with boiling water. If the meat is placed in cold water and allowed to come to a boil, the meat juices will enrich the broth and the broth will be more flavorful than the meat. If the meat is covered with boiling water, the meat will retain more of its juices making the meat tastier and more tender.

- 2 pounds beef shank with bone
- 2 pounds veal neck bones
- 2 marrow bones
- 2 turkey wings, *or* 1 turkey leg
- 2 carrots, halved
- 2 onions, quartered
- 2 stalks celery, halved
- 10 sprigs Italian flat-leaf parsley
- ½ teaspoon whole peppercorns
- Salt to taste

Wash the meats, place in a stock pot. Add enough cold water to cover the meats plus 4 inches and bring to a boil. Skim the scum from the surface, add the vegetables, peppercorns, and some salt and bring back to a boil. Lower the heat, cover, and cook at a very slow simmer for 4 hours.

Cool the broth in the pot, strain and refrigerate. When ready to use, remove the solidified fat and proceed with your recipe. The meat can be boned and served hot or cold with *salsa verde* (green sauce, page 121) or made into *polpettine* (meat patties, page 98).

CHICKEN BROTH
Brodo di Pollo

Makes about 2 quarts

Broth for the holidays was traditionally made with capon which is considered more flavorful than chicken and more festive to present at the table as they are plumper and larger than the average chicken. A good chicken broth is enriched with a variety of meats including chicken, hens, and turkey. The combination of a chicken or hen with the addition of easily available turkey wings or legs makes a wonderfully rich and flavorful broth.

- 1 (3 to 4 pounds) chicken, fowl, or capon
- 2 turkey wings or a turkey leg
- 1 carrot, halved
- 1 onion or leek, quartered
- 1 stalk celery, halved
- 5 sprigs Italian flat-leaf parsley
- 6 fresh mushrooms, *or* ½ ounce dry porcini mushrooms
- Salt to taste

Wash the poultry, place in a stock pot, cover with water plus 4 inches and bring to a boil. Skim the scum from the surface, add the washed vegetables and salt, bring back to a boil, lower the heat, cover and simmer for 4 hours.

Let the broth cool and then strain. Refrigerate the broth and remove the solidified fat before using. What you don't use in a few days can be frozen. Bone the poultry and use for *polpettine* (meat patties, page 98).

RICOTTA CUBES IN BROTH

"Royal" per Il Brodo

6 to 8 servings

16 ounces fresh ricotta cheese

4 tablespoons freshly grated Parmigiano-Reggiano cheese

2 eggs

2 egg yolks

pinch of salt

½ teaspoon grated lemon zest

6 to 8 cups beef or chicken broth (pages 65 or 66), brought to a boil

Preheat oven to 350 degrees. Mix the ricotta cheese with a wooden spoon until smooth. Add the rest of the ingredients and mix till combined.

Butter a square pyrex pan, cover the bottom with parchment paper and butter the paper. Spoon the ricotta mixture into the pan, place it in a roasting pan, pour enough water into the roasting pan to reach halfway up the sides of the square pan. Bake in the preheated 350-degree oven for 45 minutes.

Cool cheese in the pan, unmold, remove the parchment paper, and cut into ½-inch cubes. Place the ricotta cubes in a soup tureen and pour boiling broth on top. Alternately, distribute the cubes among 4 or 6 soup plates and add the boiling broth to each.

BEAN SOUP
Minestra di Fagioli

8 to 10 servings

¼ cup olive oil, plus more to drizzle

2 ounces pancetta, cubed

battuto: 1 carrot, 1 onion, and 2 ribs celery, chopped together

8 ounces tomato puree

8 ounces dried *borlotti* (cranberry) beans, soaked overnight; *or* 2 pounds fresh *borlotti* beans, shelled

salt to taste

2 cups *maltagliati* (page 36)

½ cup (2 ounces) freshly grated Parmigiano-Reggiano cheese

Heat the ¼ cup of olive oil in a large pot, add the pancetta and cook until it begins to color. Add the *battuto* and stir-fry until it begins to turn golden and fragrant. Add the tomato puree and drained beans (fresh or soaked) and 2 quarts (8 cups) of water. Bring to a boil, lower the heat, cover and simmer for 1½ to 2 hours.

When the beans are soft, add salt to taste. Mash some of the beans right in the pot to thicken the soup, add the pasta, and cook another 5 minutes. Serve with freshly grated Parmigiano-Reggiano cheese and a drizzle of extra virgin olive oil.

VEGETARIAN SOUP

Minestra di Verdure

8 to 10 servings

- ¼ cup olive oil, plus more to drizzle
- 2 carrots, chopped
- 2 onions, chopped
- 2 stalks celery, chopped
- 8 ounces tomato puree (fresh or canned)
- 2 baking potatoes, cubed
- ½ head Savoy cabbage, shredded
- salt and pepper to taste
- 2 zucchini, quartered lengthwise and chopped
- 8 ounces dried ditalini pasta
- ½ cup (2 ounces) freshly grated Parmigiano-Reggiano cheese

Heat the olive oil in a large pot, add the chopped carrots, onions, and celery and stir-fry until you can smell its fragrance. Add the tomato puree, stir to mix, and add 2 quarts (8 cups) of water. Bring to a boil. Add the potatoes, cabbage, and salt and pepper to taste. Bring back to a boil, lower the heat, cover and simmer for 50 minutes.

Add the zucchini and pasta, and cook for another 10 minutes. Serve with a drizzle of extra virgin olive oil and freshly grated Parmigiano-Reggiano.

COLD MINESTRONE
Minestrone Freddo

8 to 10 servings

This is a very simple preparation and the finished soup is light and easy to digest because of the absence of cooked fat. Favored in summer at room temperature, it's equally delicious piping hot topped with grated cheese; in both cases the drizzle of olive oil at the table is a must.

2 potatoes, cubed

2 carrots, cubed

1 pound green beans, cut into pieces

1 pound swiss chard, *or* 1 10-ounce bag fresh spinach, coarsely shredded

1 pound *borlotti* (cranberry) beans (either fresh, canned, or dried, soaked overnight)

1 teaspoon salt

10 basil leaves, finely shredded

½ cup (2 ounces) freshly grated Parmigiano-Reggiano cheese

¼ cup extra virgin olive oil

Bring 2 quarts (8 cups) of cold water to a boil. Add all the vegetables and the salt. Bring back to a boil, lower the heat and simmer for 1 hour.

Mash the vegetables with a potato masher to thicken the broth while keeping the chunky texture of the soup. When the soup is finished cooking, turn off the heat, add the basil, stir, and let stand until room temperature. Pour into a tureen, add the Parmigiano-Reggiano and the olive oil, stir and serve.

This soup can also be served hot and is delicious topped with crostini. (Toast one or two slices of bread per serving, and while the bread is still hot, top with a sprinkling of grated Parmigiano-Reggiano.)

PUREED SOUP
Minestra Passata

6 to 8 servings

4 ounces pancetta, cubed

battuto: 1 onion, 1 carrot, 2 stalks celery, chopped together

4 potatoes, peeled, washed and cubed

1 leek, carefully washed and chopped

8 ounces fresh mushrooms, sliced with the stems

½ ounce dried porcini mushrooms, soaked, rinsed, and chopped

salt and pepper to taste

½ cup (2 ounces) freshly grated Parmigiano-Reggiano cheese

Put the pancetta in a soup pot and place over low heat to begin to render its fat. Add the *battuto* and cook until the vegetables are soft and fragrant. Add 2 quarts (8 cups) of water, bring to a boil, add the potatoes, leek, mushrooms, dried mushrooms with their liquid, and salt and pepper to taste. Lower the heat to a simmer, cover and cook for 45 minutes.

Turn off the heat and let the soup stand for 30 minutes. Puree the soup with an immersion blender or in batches in a food processor. Top each portion with a drizzle of extra virgin olive oil and a *nevicata* or "snowfall" of freshly grated Parmigiano-Reggiano.

MINESTRONE MODENA-STYLE

Minestrone di Modena

8 to 10 servings

This is the original fast food since it keeps well in the refrigerator and will be enough for several meals. You can vary it by serving the soup topped with crostini with melted Parmigiano-Reggiano or ladled over a slice of plain toasted bread.

1 ounce dried porcini mushrooms

¼ cup extra virgin olive oil

2 ounces butter

4 ounces pancetta, cubed

battuto: ½ onion, 1 carrot, 1 stalk celery, all finely chopped together

8 ounces dried *borlotti* (cranberry) or cannellini beans, soaked and drained

1½ onions, chopped

2 carrots, cubed

2 stalks celery, sliced

2 tomatoes, peeled and chopped

½ pound fresh mushrooms, sliced

2 potatoes, peeled and diced

½ pound green beans, cut into small pieces

½ head savoy cabbage, chopped

piece of cheese rind, if available

Soak the dried mushrooms for 30 minutes in 1 cup of warm water. Drain, reserving the liquid, rinse well, chop, and set aside.

Heat the olive oil and butter in a large pot. Add the pancetta and fry until it begins to render its fat. Add the *battuto* and soaked porcini mushrooms and stir-fry until the vegetables are limp and fragrant but not brown. Add the pre-soaked beans, onions, carrots, celery, tomatoes, mushrooms, potatoes, green beans, and savoy cabbage and stir for 2 minutes.

Add 2 quarts (8 cups) of water to cover the vegetables plus a few inches. Add the cheese rind, if available, and salt and pepper to taste and bring to a boil; lower the heat, cover, and simmer for 1½ hours.

Add the zucchini, peas, and pasta and cook for 7 to 10 more minutes. Add the shredded basil leaves, if using, turn off the heat and let the soup rest for 30 minutes. Serve with freshly grated Parmigiano-Reggiano cheese.

salt and pepper to taste

2 zucchini, quartered lengthwise and sliced

1 10-ounce package frozen tender tiny peas, defrosted

1 cup small dried pasta (such as ditalini)

6 fresh basil leaves, shredded (optional)

freshly grated Parmigiano-Reggiano cheese

CHESTNUT SOUP
Minestra di Castagne

4 to 6 servings

Chestnut Soup is a delicious comfort food. My friend Annamaria Clerici makes a quicker version by simply boiling pre-soaked dried chestnuts, draining and serving them whole in a bowl of warm milk as a refreshing light supper which was and still is a favorite of her niece Annamaria Agnetti.

- 4 tablespoons butter
- 1 onion, chopped
- 1 stalk celery, thinly sliced
- 1 carrot, chopped
- 2 leeks, carefully washed and chopped
- 8 ounces dried chestnuts, soaked overnight
- 2 cups whole or lowfat milk
- salt to taste
- freshly grated Parmigiano-Reggiano cheese

Heat the butter in a large pot. Add the onion, celery, carrot, and leeks and stir-fry until softened but not browned. Add 6 cups water and bring to a boil. Lower the heat, add the soaked chestnuts and continue to cook over low heat for 60 minutes.

Remove and set aside enough whole chestnuts to serve 2 on each portion of soup. Puree the soup with an immersion blender or in a food processor. Add the milk and heat through. Season with salt to taste, and serve hot with freshly grated Parmigiano-Reggiano cheese.

RICE AND CHESTNUT MINESTRONE

Minestrone di Riso e Castagne

4 to 6 servings

- 4 ounces (about ¾ cup) dried chestnuts
- 4 tablespoons extra virgin olive oil
- 2 ounces pancetta, finely chopped
- *battuto*: 1 onion, 1 carrot, 1 stalk celery, 4 sprigs Italian flat-leaf parsley, finely chopped together
- 6 cups chicken broth
- salt and pepper to taste
- ¾ cup arborio rice

Soak the chestnuts in cold water overnight.

Drain the chestnuts, place in a pot, add 6 cups cold water, bring to a boil, lower the heat to a simmer, cover and cook for 1 hour or until soft. Set aside the chestnuts and the broth they were cooked in until needed.

Heat the olive oil in a large pot, add the pancetta and *battuto* and cook until the vegetables are soft but not browned. Add the chicken broth, cooked chestnuts with their cooking broth, and salt and pepper to taste. Bring to a boil, add the rice, bring back to a boil, lower the heat, cover and simmer for 20 minutes, or until rice is tender.

MOLDED PASTA, DUMPLINGS, RICE & POLENTA

Timballi, Gnocchi, Riso e Polenta

TIMBALLI, GNOCCHI, RISO E POLENTA
MOLDED PASTA, DUMPLINGS, RICE & POLENTA

BAKED PASTA FERRARA-STYLE

Timballo alla Ferrarese

6 to 8 servings

SWEET PASTA *FROLLA*:

¼ cup lard, shortening, or butter

2½ cups all-purpose flour

pinch of salt

2 tablespoons sugar

1 egg plus 1 egg yolk (reserve the egg white to brush on the top crust)

2 to 6 tablespoons cold water

FILLING:

1 pound penne pasta

3 cups Bolognese sauce (page 125)

1½ cups freshly grated Parmigiano-Reggiano cheese

4 tablespoons butter, divided

2 cups béchamel sauce (page 123)

Make the dough (by hand or in a food processor): cut the lard, shortening, or butter into the flour; add the salt, sugar, egg, egg yolk, and enough water to make a soft dough. Wrap in plastic and place in the refrigerator while you prepare the filling.

Cook the penne pasta until barely soft since it will finish cooking in the oven. Drain and mix with 2 cups of the Bolognese sauce and 1 cup of grated Parmigiano-Reggiano cheese.

Preheat the oven to 375 degrees. Divide the dough into 3 portions: use 2 portions for the bottom crust and one for the top. Roll the bottom crust into a circle that will fit into a large springform pan allowing a 2-inch overhang all around. Roll the top crust to a circle the diameter of the pan.

Butter a large springform pan with 2 tablespoons of the butter, line it with the bottom crust letting it overhang by 2 inches. Spoon ⅓ of the pasta mixture on top of the crust, top with ⅓ of the remaining Bolognese sauce, ⅓ of the béchamel sauce, and ⅓ of the grated Parmigiano-Reggiano cheese. Make 2 more layers in the same manner. Dot the top with the remaining 2 tablespoons of butter. Cover with the top crust, fold the overhang of the bottom crust over the top, brush with the reserved egg white and prick with a fork. Bake in the preheated 375-degree oven for 40 to 50 minutes. Let rest for 15 to 30 minutes before cutting.

POTATO DUMPLINGS

Gnocchi di Patate

4 to 6 servings

4 baking potatoes
1 egg
2 tablespoons unsalted butter, at room temperature
¾ to 1 cup all-purpose flour
good pinch of salt

Wash the potatoes, place in a pot, cover with cold water plus 2 inches, bring to a boil, lower the heat and cook for 40 to 50 minutes or until soft. While still hot, peel and rice the potatoes. Allow to cool.

When the potatoes are cool enough to handle, add the egg, butter, and flour and mix into a soft but not sticky dough. Working with a bench scraper on a floured surface, divide the dough into 4 parts. Roll each part into a long thin cylinder the width of a finger and cut into 1-inch pieces. Using a butter paddle or a fork, lightly press and roll each piece to make the traditional ridges. Cover a tray or a jelly roll pan with a towel, sprinkle with flour and place the finished gnocchi on it to dry until ready to cook.

Using a low, wide pot or a chef's pan, bring 2 quarts (8 cups) of water to a boil. Add 1 teaspoon salt and carefully add the gnocchi. When they rise to the surface, remove from the water with a skimmer and place in a serving platter. Serve with melted butter and freshly grated Parmigiano-Reggiano cheese, or with Bolognese sauce (page 125) or your favorite sauce.

RICE SALAD

Insalata di Riso

6 to 8 servings

This is a classic summer dish that can be endlessly enriched with meats, cheeses, and vegetables that you already have on hand and simply dressed with olive oil. Generally there's no need to add salt or vinegar since some of the ingredients already add salt, spice, and vinegar to the salad.

- 2 cups arborio rice
- 1 thick slice prosciutto or baked ham, cut into cubes; *or* 6 ounces tuna, packed in olive oil
- ¼ cup pitted olives, each cut in half
- ½ cup *giardiniera* (Italian pickled vegetables), chopped; *or* 2 pickles, chopped
- 1 cup cooked fresh peas; *or* ½ a 10-ounce package frozen tender tiny peas, just defrosted
- Optional: roasted red peppers, chopped (for color and flavor)
- ¼ cup extra virgin olive oil

Steam or boil the rice until tender. Drain and allow to cool.

Mix the cooled rice gently with all the ingredients except the oil. Pour on the olive oil, toss gently and serve.

MOLDED RICE
Bomba di Riso

6 to 8 servings

This is an ancient dish traditionally made with pigeon or squab, but it's equally flavorful made with readily available Cornish hens. Our dear friend Isabella Silva Musa continued to make a deliciously flavorful Bomba di Riso *after she left her native Parma for Bloomington, Indiana, where she hosted delightful dinner parties for friends and colleagues of her husband, Dr. Mark Musa, who was Distinguished Professor of Italian and Dante Scholar at Indiana University.*

RICE:

2 cups meat broth (page 65)

2 cups arborio rice

2 eggs

2 tablespoons pan juices from the cooked hens

1 cup (4 ounces) freshly grated Parmigiano-Reggiano cheese

CORNISH HENS:

2 tablespoons butter

battuto: 1 onion, 1 carrot, finely chopped together

2 Cornish hens, quartered; *or* 6 squabs, left whole; *or* 2 pigeons, quartered

Livers from the Cornish hens, squabs, or pigeons, cleaned, washed, and chopped

1 tablespoon tomato paste

Bring the meat broth to a boil in a medium pot, add the rice, stir, lower the heat and cook, stirring very often, for 12 minutes, or until the broth is absorbed by the rice but the rice is still al dente. Cover and let rest while you cook the meat.

Heat the butter in a large deep skillet and add the *battuto* and cook until the onion is limp and the *battuto* is fragrant. Add the hens and chopped livers and brown. Add the tomato paste to a hot spot in the pan and cook for a few minutes. Add the white wine and allow the meat to absorb it. As the wine reduces, add ¼ cup hot broth at a time to keep the meat moist. Add salt and pepper to taste, reduce the heat, cover the pan and simmer for 30 minutes or until the meat is tender, adding the remainder of the broth if necessary so that the sauce does not dry out.

Remove the hens, debone, return the meat to the pan, and continue cooking in the pan juices for 10 more minutes. Remove from the heat and set aside until ready to use.

½ cup white wine
1 cup meat broth (page 65)
½ cup breadcrumbs

Preheat oven to 350 degrees. Butter a 10-inch to 11-inch glass or stainless steel bowl and coat with breadcrumbs. Mix the cold rice with the eggs, pan juices, and grated Parmigiano-Reggiano.

Carefully pack two-thirds of the rice on the bottom and up the sides of the bowl making a thick coating of rice in the mold. Fill the cavity with the meat using a slotted spoon and reserving the juices in the pan. Cover the meat with the rest of the rice and spread evenly. Sprinkle with breadcrumbs.

Bake for 30 minutes until a light crust forms. Remove from the oven and let rest for 15 minutes before turning the mold over on a serving platter. Serve in wedges with the reserved pan juices.

RISOTTO WITH MUSHROOMS

Risotto ai Funghi

6 to 8 servings

8 cups beef or chicken broth (pages 65, 66)

½ ounce dried porcini mushrooms

6 tablespoons butter, divided

1 onion, chopped

2 cups arborio rice

salt to taste

¾ cup (3 ounces) freshly grated Parmigiano-Reggiano cheese

Bring the broth to a boil in a large saucepan, lower the heat and keep at a simmer. Meanwhile place the mushrooms in a bowl, cover with hot water, let soak for 20 minutes; strain, reserving the liquid, rinse the mushrooms, chop and set aside.

Heat 3 tablespoons butter in a large saucepan. Add the chopped onion and cook until softened. Add the mushrooms and stir-fry for 2 minutes. Add the rice and stir to blend the flavors and coat the grains with the butter. Add some salt, the mushroom liquid, and ½ cup of hot broth; continue stirring until the broth is absorbed by the rice. Keep stirring and adding broth as the rice absorbs it until the rice is tender, about 18 to 20 minutes.

Remove the rice from the heat, add the remaining butter and the grated Parmigiano-Reggiano and serve piping hot.

POLENTA

6 to 8 servings

For some, polenta is best when served hot and soft, simply dotted with plenty of butter and topped with freshly grated Parmigiano-Reggiano cheese. It can also be topped with meat or vegetable stews. The leftovers can be sliced and grilled, baked, or fried into an entirely new dish the next day.

- 1 teaspoon salt
- 1½ cups Italian polenta (medium ground yellow cornmeal)
- 4 tablespoons butter

Bring 6 cups of water to a boil in a large pot, add the salt and sprinkle in the cornmeal while energetically whisking to prevent lumps. Once all the cornmeal has been added, start stirring with a wooden spoon and continue cooking over low heat until the polenta had thickened and the cornmeal is cooked, about 40 to 45 minutes. Turn off the heat, stir in the butter and serve.

POLENTA WITH STEWED MUSHROOMS

Polenta con Spezzatino di Funghi

6 to 8 servings

- 1 recipe polenta (page 87)
- 2 tablespoons butter
- 2 tablespoons olive oil
- 1 onion, chopped
- 6 sprigs Italian flat-leaf parsley, chopped
- 2 pounds button, cremini, shitake, and/or portobello mushrooms in any available proportion, washed and sliced
- salt and freshly ground pepper to taste
- 1 cup heavy cream

Prepare the polenta according to the recipe on page 87.

Meanwhile, heat the butter and olive oil in a large skillet, add the onion and cook until just beginning to color. Add the parsley and stir. Add the fresh sliced mushrooms, salt and pepper to taste, and cook uncovered for 10 to 15 minutes or until tender. Add the cream and cook and stir till hot.

Place the polenta in a serving dish, top with the stewed mushrooms and serve.

BAKED POLENTA
Polenta Pasticciata

6 to 8 servings

This delicious one-dish meal is generally reserved for leftover polenta, which is sliced and layered with leftover meats, vegetables, or cheeses and a flavorful sauce in an ovenproof pan and then baked to heat through. It can also be prepared with freshly made polenta, a quick sauce, a sprinkling of cheese, and a little butter.

4 tablespoons butter, divided

1 recipe hot polenta (page 87); *or* the equivalent in cold sliced polenta

1½ cups tomato sauce (page 121, 124, or 125); *or* 1½ cups béchamel sauce (page 123)

¾ cup (3 ounces) freshly grated Parmigiano-Reggiano cheese

Preheat oven to 350 degrees. Butter a 9-by-12-inch pyrex baking dish that can be brought to the table with 1 tablespoon of the butter.

Make a layer of fresh polenta or leftover slices in the baking dish, top with ½ cup of the tomato or béchamel sauce, ¼ cup of Parmigiano-Reggiano, and dot with 1 tablespoon of the butter. Make 2 more layers, ending with the remaining sauce, cheese, and butter.

Bake in the 350-degree oven for 20 to 25 minutes or until bubbly and heated through. Let stand for 10 minutes and serve.

POLENTA WITH MUSHROOM AND SAUSAGE SAUCE

Polenta con Salsa di Funghi e Salsiccie

6 to 8 servings

1 recipe polenta (page 87)

MUSHROOM AND SAUSAGE SAUCE:

½ cup dried porcini mushrooms

2 tablespoons butter

2 tablespoons olive oil

2 pounds Italian sausage, cut into ½-inch slices

1 onion, chopped

½ cup red Lambrusco wine

6 ounces Italian tomato paste

1 cup beef or chicken broth (pages 65, 66)

salt and pepper to taste

½ cup (2 ounces) freshly grated Parmigiano-Reggiano cheese

Soak the dried mushrooms in 1 cup hot water for 30 minutes. Drain, reserving the water, rinse and chop coarsely.

Heat the butter and olive oil, add the sliced sausage and brown. Remove the sausage from the pan and set aside.

Add the chopped onion to the pan drippings and cook until soft. Add the chopped porcini mushrooms and stir-fry for 2 minutes. Add the wine and reduce for another 2 minutes.

Dissolve the tomato paste in the broth and add to the pan together with the browned sausage and the mushroom soaking liquid. Add salt and pepper to taste, lower the heat and simmer for 30 minutes, stirring occasionally.

Spoon the sauce over the hot polenta and top with the freshly grated Parmigiano-Reggiano.

MAIN DISHES

Secondi Piatti

SECONDI PIATTI
MAIN DISHES

COLD MEATLOAF
Polpettone Freddo

6 to 8 servings

This is an unusual boiled dish as it is served cold with salsa verde *and* cetriolini *(green sauce and cornichons). It was made for us by our dear friend Pina Franceschini Cagna when we visited her in Berceto. Her husband, Rino, had his own specialty that was served after Pina's delicious dinner.* Nocino *is a typical walnut cordial from Emilia-Romagna that Rino still made each year at home, adhering to the tradition of picking the green walnuts on the evening of June 24th, the feast of Saint John the Baptist, when the immature walnuts are thought to be just perfect to make this regional treat.*

- 1½ pounds beef, ground twice
- 2 eggs
- ½ cup (2 ounces) freshly grated Parmigiano-Reggiano cheese
- ½ teaspoon salt
- ¼ teaspoon pepper
- a grind of nutmeg (about ¼ teaspoon)

Ask the butcher to grind the beef twice for a finer texture. Mix the ground beef, eggs, Parmigiano-Reggiano, salt, pepper, and nutmeg until well combined. Shape into a thick roll and wrap in 2 thicknesses of cheesecloth (being careful to overlap the ends of the cheesecloth to completely enclose the meat) and tie both ends securely with cotton twine.

Place the meatloaf in a pot that will fit it comfortably or in a fish poacher, cover with boiling water, lower the heat, cover, and simmer for 30 minutes.

Cool the meat roll in its broth. Remove the roll from the pot, reserve the broth for soup, slice the meat thickly and serve with *salsa verde* (green sauce, page 121).

MIXED BOILED DINNER
Bollito Misto

8 to 12 servings

This classic company dinner yields wonderful meats and a deliciously rich broth that can be served with* tagliatelle, tortellini, *any of the stuffed pastas, or* passatelli. Cappone *or capon (a castrated rooster) was traditionally added to the* bollito misto, *but a chicken can be substituted. A variety of meats such as poultry, beef, veal, and pork yield the quintessential* Gran Bollito Misto *for important holidays, when family and friends share this deceptively simple and simply delicious culinary feast.

NOTE: The procedure for measuring the amount of water needed to cook all the meats and to also make a good broth for soup is to place all the meats except the *cotechino* sausage (which is cooked separately) in a stockpot, cover the meats with cold water plus 4 inches, and then remove the meats from the cold water and leave at room temperature as they do in Italy or refrigerate until ready to drop each into the boiling water. For boiled meat to be succulent and tender it must be added to boiling water so that the heat seals in its juices.

- 1-to-2-pound chuck roast or shin of beef with or without the bone
- 1 to 2 pounds boneless veal
- 1 to 2 pounds veal tongue
- 2-to-3-pound capon or chicken, stuffed if preferred (see recipe page 99)
- 3 sprigs Italian flat-leaf parsley
- 2 bay leaves
- ½ teaspoon whole peppercorns

Bring the necessary amount of water to a boil in a large stockpot (see note). Add some salt and lower the beef into the pot. Bring back to a boil, skim the surface to remove any scum, lower the heat to a bare simmer, cover and cook the beef for 1½ hours.

Add the veal, tongue, and poultry. Bring back to a boil, skim the surface to remove any scum, add the parsley, bay leaves, peppercorns, some salt, and the vegetables and continue to cook for 1½ to 2 hours or until the meats are very tender.

salt to taste

6 onions, peeled and each studded with 1 whole clove

6 carrots

8 stalks celery, each cut in half

1 to 2 pounds *cotechino* sausage

Meanwhile, cook the *cotechino*: Place the *cotechino* in a separate pot or in a fish poacher that would fit it very comfortably. Cover with cold water, bring to a boil, lower the heat and simmer gently for 1 to 1½ hours or until cooked. If the *cotechino* is pre-cooked (it will say on the label) it only needs to simmer for 30 minutes, just to heat through. When ready to serve, remove from the pot, discard the cooking water, remove the casing and cut into thick slices.

Leave the meats in their broth until ready to eat, then drain the meats and reserve the broth. (Refrigerate the broth and remove the accumulated fat before using it for soups, stews, or sauces.) Slice the beef roast. Remove and discard the skin from the tongue and slice. Remove the casing from the *cotechino* and slice. Cut the chicken into serving pieces together with the stuffing.

Arrange the variety of meats on a great big platter (with handles if you wish to make a grand entrance as you carry it to the dining table). There is nothing more festive and satisfying than this abundance of fragrant and flavorful meats. Serve with *salsa verde* (green sauce, page 121), savory zabaglione sauce (page 100), and *mostarda* (Italian preserved fruit).

MEAT PATTIES
Polpettine

6 to 8 servings

This is a variant using bollito misto *or boiled meats to make delicious and flavorful patties, browned and crispy on the outside and tender on the inside, which are served hot as a* secondo *or main dish after the soup.*

- Cooked meat from *Brodo di Carne* (page 65) or *Brodo di Pollo* (page 66), coarsely ground
- ½ cup (2 ounces) freshly grated Parmigiano-Reggiano cheese
- 1 egg
- 6 sprigs Italian flat-leaf parsley, finely chopped
- salt and pepper to taste
- ¼ cup olive oil for frying

Mix all the ingredients except the oil and shape into patties. Heat the oil in a frying pan and fry the patties until browned on both sides, about 5 to 7 minutes. Serve accompanied by a salad.

STUFFED CAPON
Cappone Ripieno

6 to 8 servings

This stuffed capon can be cooked as part of the bollito misto *(page 96) or separately for a delicious Sunday dinner.*

2-to-3 pound capon

STUFFING:

6 tablespoons butter

2 onions, chopped

4 cups freshly made coarse breadcrumbs

1 cup hot milk

2 eggs, beaten

½-inch-thick slice of mortadella, cut into small cubes

¾ cup (3 ounces) freshly grated Parmigiano-Reggiano cheese

½ teaspoon salt

¼ teaspoon pepper

¼ teaspoon freshly grated nutmeg

Heat the butter in a large saucepan, add the onion and cook until softened. Remove from the heat, add the breadcrumbs. Pour the hot milk over the crumbs to moisten and quickly mix to combine. Add the eggs to bind the stuffing and let stand 15 minutes. Add the cubed mortadella, Parmigiano-Reggiano cheese, salt, pepper and nutmeg and mix well. Fill the capon, close the opening with toothpicks, and then lace around the toothpicks with kitchen twine.

To boil the capon: Carefully place the stuffed capon into a pot of boiling water, lower the heat, cover and simmer for 1½ to 2 hours, depending on the size of the bird. Remove from the pot, cover with aluminum foil and a towel until ready to eat. Serve hot and use the broth for soups.

To roast the capon: If you wish to roast the stuffed capon, brush the entire surface with melted butter, sprinkle with salt, place in a roasting pan on a rack. Pour 2 cups water in the bottom of the pan and bake in a preheated 375-degree oven for 1¼ to 1½ hours or until the skin is crisp and golden. Remove from the oven, let rest for 15 to 30 minutes before serving with the pan juices.

SAUSAGE WITH ZABAGLIONE SAUCE

Cotechino con Zabaglione

4 to 6 servings

Although zabaglione sauce is not a classic accompaniment to cotechino*, it has become a common combination that enhances the flavor of the sweet* cotechino *sausage and makes a beautiful presentation. If served alone, place the* cotechino *on a serving platter partially sliced with the overlapping slices surrounded by the zabaglione which will cover the base of the platter. This sauce, which is served cold, is a good substitute for homemade mayonnaise which some people find objectionable since it uses raw eggs. If the* cotechino *is cooked as part of the* Bollito Misto *(**page 96**), serve the sauce separately and it'll be delicious on some of the other meats as well.*

1 to 2 pounds *cotechino* sausage

ZABAGLIONE SAUCE:

4 egg yolks

½ cup white wine

salt to taste

a grinding of fresh nutmeg

Cook the *cotechino*: Place the *cotechino* in a pot or fish poacher that fits it very comfortably. Cover with cold water, bring to a boil, lower the heat and simmer gently for 1 to 1½ hours or until cooked. If the *cotechino* is pre-cooked (it will say on the label) it only needs to simmer for 30 minutes, just to heat through. When ready to serve, remove from the pot, discard the cooking water, remove the casing and cut into thick slices.

Place the egg yolks in a double boiler or a metal bowl placed over a small pan of simmering water and whisk until thick and light. Add the wine and seasonings and continue to whisk over simmering water until the mixture forms a ribbon when the whisk is raised and the zabaglione falls back into the pot or bowl.

Cool the sauce and serve either around the sliced *cotechino* or in a separate bowl to pass around at the table.

SAUSAGE WITH LENTILS
Cotechino con Lenticchie

6 to 8 servings

This is a traditional New Year's Day dinner because the coin-shaped lentils symbolize prosperity and the rich sausage stands for good luck and well being for the new year, but it is also enjoyed throughout the winter.

- ½ pound dry lentils
- 4 ounces Italian pancetta, cubed
- salt and pepper to taste
- 1 *cotechino* sausage

Pick over the lentils, wash, place in a pot, and add 2 quarts (8 cups) of water. Bring to a boil, lower the heat and simmer for 8 minutes. Turn off the heat and let stand for at least 1 hour or even overnight.

Cook the *cotechino*: Place the *cotechino* in a pot or fish poacher that fits it very comfortably. Cover with cold water, bring to a boil, lower the heat and simmer gently for 1 to 1½ hours or until cooked. If the *cotechino* is pre-cooked (it will say on the label) it only needs to simmer for 30 minutes, just to heat through. When ready to serve, remove from the pot, discard the cooking water, remove the casing and cut into thick slices.

When ready to eat remove most of the lentils from the pot with a skimmer and set aside. (Reserve the broth and some of the lentils for soup to which you can add *maltagliati* pasta, then drizzle with extra virgin olive oil at the table.)

Heat a frying pan, add the cubed pancetta, and cook until it just begins to crisp up. Add the cooked lentils and salt and pepper to taste, stir to distribute the flavors, and heat through. Place the lentils on a serving platter and arrange the slices of *cotechino* around the lentils. You can also serve the *cotechino* in a separate platter, with the overlapping slices placed on a bed of cold zabaglione (see opposite page).

IMPRISONED COTECHINO

Cotechino in Galera

6 to 8 servings

Pellegrino Artusi, a native of Emilia-Romagna, was the author of what is considered the first Italian cookbook with traditional national and regional recipes. L'Arte di Mangiare Bene *(The Art of Eating Well), published in 1891, quickly became a classic and remains a bestseller to this day. This Artusi recipe is hearty and delicious accompanied by mashed potatoes or polenta. A fish poacher is very useful to cook the* cotechino *without having to use a large amount of water which would dilute the flavors.*

- 1 ounce dried porcini mushrooms, soaked in hot water
- 1 *cotechino* sausage
- large slice of beef for *brasciole*, pounded thin
- 2 tablespoons butter
- *battuto*: 1 onion, 1 carrot, 1 stalk celery, chopped together
- 1 cup red Lambrusco wine

Soak the dried mushrooms in hot water for 30 minutes. Drain the mushrooms, reserving water, and rinse and chop. Strain the soaking water and set aside.

Boil the *cotechino* whether raw or fully cooked for 15 minutes to remove the casing. Wrap the *cotechino* in the beef, tie securely with kitchen twine.

Melt the butter in a deep skillet and brown the meat on all sides. Add the *battuto* and stir until softened and fragrant. Add the wine, stir, turn the meat to flavor all over. Salt lightly since the *cotechino* is already well flavored. After most of the wine has evaporated add the mushrooms and the reserved soaking liquid together with enough water to reach halfway up the meat. Lower the heat to a simmer, cover, and cook slowly for 1 hour.

Let the meat rest for at least 15 minutes. Remove the string, carve into thick slices and serve over mashed potatoes or soft polenta topped with the pan juices.

BRAISED BEEF FROM PARMA

Stracotto di Parma

6 to 8 servings

Our dear friend Isabella Musa remembers her mother cooking the stracotto *no less than 24 hours, although she now agrees that with better temperature controls the cooking time can be drastically reduced. Isabella brought the rich cooking and elegance of her native Parma to the United States when she first arrived at The Johns Hopkins University in Baltimore where her young husband, Mark Musa, was completing his Ph.D. in Romance Languages.* Stracotto *is a classic dish that yields the pan juices used to make delicious* anolini, *a small filled pasta served in rich capon broth.*

- 2 tablespoons butter
- 2½ pounds beef (London broil)
- 2 ounces pancetta, chopped
- *battuto*: 2 onions, 2 carrots, 2 ribs of celery, finely chopped together
- 2 cups red wine (Lambrusco is the favorite, but Barolo or Barbaresco are also delicious)
- meat broth (page 65)
- salt and pepper to taste

Heat the butter in a heavy-bottomed pot or Dutch oven. Add the beef, brown on all sides, remove and set aside. Add the pancetta, cook for two minutes, then add the *battuto* and cook until it begins to color and becomes fragrant. Return the beef to the pot, add ½ cup of the wine and turn the beef to flavor on all sides as the wine evaporates. Barely cover the beef with broth and add salt and pepper to taste. Reduce to a very slow simmer and cook for 6 hours, adding ¼ cup of wine every hour until the meat is thoroughly cooked and the juices are richly flavored. Keep an eye on the pot, and add small amounts of boiling water if the liquids should reduce too much.

Turn off the heat, remove the meat and puree the pan juices with the vegetables to thicken using an immersion blender. Set aside 1½ cups of the *stracotto* juices to make *anolini* filling (page 58) and serve the rest over the sliced pot roast, or, using 2 forks, shred the beef into its juices and use as a delicious sauce for *tagliatelle* or gnocchi.

STUFFED VEAL
Vitello Farcito

6 to 8 servings

This is the special recipe of my friend Anna Maria Clerici who works miracles in her compact kitchen in the beautiful hill town of Berceto in the province of Parma. Anna Maria makes this the day before so that it's easier to get perfect slices. When ready to serve, she heats the pan juices, adds the slices to heat them through and serves the meat with its own sauce. I serve it freshly roasted after a 30-minute rest period.

2-pound veal roast, butterflied and pounded thin
2 slices mortadella
2 tablespoons extra virgin olive oil
2 tablespoons butter
juice of 1 lemon
1 cup white wine
salt and pepper to taste

FRITTATA:
2 eggs
2 sprigs parsley
pinch each of salt and pepper
2 tablespoons extra virgin olive oil

Make the frittata: Beat the eggs with the parsley, salt, and pepper. Heat the olive oil in a 12-inch skillet, pour the egg mixture in the pan, tilting to be sure that the eggs cover the bottom of the pan. When cooked on one side, turn the frittata to cook the other side. Remove to a plate and set aside.

Place the veal on the counter, cover it with slices of mortadella and top with the frittata making sure the mortadella and frittata cover the entire piece of meat. Trim and fit if necessary. Carefully roll the roast and tie securely in several places.

Heat the oil and butter in a pan which will hold the veal comfortably (I use a fish poacher) and brown evenly all over. Add the lemon juice and white wine, turn the meat to flavor it all around, then add enough boiling water to reach halfway up the piece of meat and some salt and pepper to taste, lower the heat to a simmer, cover and cook for 1½ to 2 hours. Check from time to time to be sure it hasn't dried out, and add small quantities of boiling water if necessary.

Cover the roast and allow it to cool for 30 minutes before cutting. Serve cut in thick slices and drizzled with the pan juices.

STUFFED MEAT ROLLS
Involtini di Carne

4 to 6 servings

Veal, beef, or pork scaloppine (thinly cut slices) can be used for this dish and are all equally delicious. Pound the meat lightly to make the slices the same even thickness.

- 8 veal, beef, or pork scaloppine, lightly pounded to even the thickness
- ½ cup (2 ounces) freshly grated Parmigiano-Reggiano cheese
- 8 thin slices prosciutto
- 2 tablespoons butter
- 2 tablespoons olive oil
- *battuto*: 1 onion, 1 carrot, 1 stalk celery, chopped together
- 1 tablespoon Italian tomato paste
- 1 cup beef or chicken broth (pages 65, 66)
- salt and pepper to taste

Place the meat on the counter, cover each scaloppine with freshly grated Parmigiano-Reggiano cheese, top each with a slice of prosciutto. Roll to enclose the filling and secure the rolls with wooden toothpicks.

Heat the butter and oil in a skillet and brown the meat rolls on all sides. Remove from the pan and set aside. Add the *battuto* to the pan and stir-fry until soft. Meanwhile, dissolve the tomato paste in the broth and set aside.

Place the meat rolls on top of the vegetables in the skillet. Add the tomato-broth mixture, cover, and simmer for 30 to 40 minutes, until the meat is cooked and the sauce has thickened nicely. Remove the toothpicks before serving.

LAMB STEW

Spezzatino D'Agnello

4 to 6 servings

- 2 pounds lamb shoulder, cut into cubes
- salt and pepper
- 3 tablespoons extra virgin olive oil
- 3 tablespoons butter
- 2 onions, chopped
- 2 sprigs fresh rosemary
- 2 bay leaves
- 2 cups red wine
- 1 cup tomato puree
- 2 pounds potatoes, cubed
- 1 10-ounce package tender tiny frozen peas

Season the lamb with salt and pepper. Heat the olive oil and butter in a heavy-bottomed pan and sear the lamb pieces on all sides. Keep the pieces separate so as not to crowd the pan. As the lamb pieces brown, remove and set aside.

Add the chopped onions and cook until they soften. Add the rosemary and bay leaves. Cook for a minute and return the browned lamb to the pot. Add the wine and reduce the liquid for 5 minutes, stirring often. Add the tomato puree and enough water to almost cover the lamb. Stir and bring to a boil. Lower the heat, cover, and simmer for 45 minutes, checking and stirring from time to time and adding additional water if necessary.

Add the potatoes and continue cooking for 40 more minutes. Add the peas and cook for another 5 minutes. Remove from the heat, spoon into a serving dish and serve over hot polenta (page 87).

OSSOBUCO ROMAGNA-STYLE

Ossobuco alla Romagnola

4 servings

4 tablespoons butter
1 small onion, chopped
4 *ossibuchi* (2-inch-thick veal shins)
salt and pepper to taste
1 cup Sangiovese wine
1 (28-ounce) can Italian plum tomatoes, pureed
a grinding of nutmeg

Heat the butter in a large saucepan, add the onion and cook until fragrant but not browned. Add the veal, sprinkle with some salt and pepper, and brown. Turn the veal, salt and pepper the other side and brown. Add the wine, reduce for a few minutes, turn the meat, and continue to cook until the wine is reduced by half.

Add the tomatoes and enough boiling water to nearly cover the meat. Add the nutmeg and bring to a boil. Lower the heat, cover and simmer for 2 hours or until the meat is very tender and the sauce has reduced and thickened. Serve with steamed rice seasoned with butter and freshly grated Parmigiano-Reggiano cheese.

GREMOLATA

(optional topping)

2 cloves garlic
bunch of Italian flat leaf parsley
zest of 1 lemon, cut into strips, or grated
salt to taste

On a medium or large chopping board, coarsely chop the garlic. Add the parsley, the lemon zest, and the salt and continue to chop until you get a fragrant, finely chopped mixture of all the ingredients. I like to chop this by hand because using the food processor would give you a paste.

Place the Ossobuco on a serving platter and sprinkle the Gremolata on top. This Gremolata is also delicious on lamb and other meats.

CHESTNUT-STUFFED CHICKEN

Pollo Ripieno di Castagne

4 to 6 servings

Chestnuts are a gift of nature. Fresh ones require some preparation to cook, peel, and remove the inner skin, but they can be purchased jarred and already prepared. Dried chestnuts are always available, and once soaked overnight and boiled can be used like fresh ones. Italians born in the middle of the twentieth century remember the flavor and sweetness of dried chestnuts as the candy of their childhood—it was a popular, delicious, and very nutritious snack.

- 1 pound fresh, cooked and shelled chestnuts; *or* 1 10-ounce jar prepared chestnuts; *or* 8 ounces dried chestnuts, soaked overnight and boiled until tender (*see opposite page*)
- 6 tablespoons butter
- 2 onions, chopped
- 2 cups freshly made coarse breadcrumbs
- ½ cup chestnut cooking water
- 1 egg
- ¾ cup (3 ounces) freshly grated Parmigiano-Reggiano cheese
- ½ teaspoon salt
- ¼ teaspoon pepper
- ¼ teaspoon freshly grated nutmeg
- 1 3-to-4-pound whole chicken

Heat the butter in a large saucepan, add the onions and cook until softened. Remove from the heat, add the breadcrumbs, moisten with the chestnut cooking water and quickly mix to combine. Add the egg to bind the stuffing and let rest for 15 minutes so that the bread can absorb the liquid. Add the Parmigiano-Reggiano cheese, salt, pepper, nutmeg, and chestnuts and mix well. Fill the cavity of the chicken with the stuffing, close the opening with toothpicks and then lace around the toothpicks with kitchen twine.

To boil the stuffed chicken: Carefully place the stuffed chicken into a pot of boiling water, lower the heat, cover and simmer for 1½ to 2 hours, depending on the size of the bird. Remove from the pot, cover with aluminum foil and a towel until ready to eat. Serve hot and use the broth for soups.

To roast the stuffed chicken: Brush the stuffed chicken with melted butter and place on a rack in a roasting pan breast up.

Pour 2 cups water into the pan and roast in a preheated 375-degree oven for 1¼ to 1½ hours or until golden brown all over. Remove from the oven and let rest for 15 to 30 minutes before carving and serving with the pan juices.

PREPARATION OF FRESH CHESTNUTS:

Cut an x on the flat side of each chestnut. Place in a pot, cover with cold water plus two inches, bring the water to a boil, lower the heat, cover and simmer 40 to 50 minutes or until soft. Reserve ½ cup of the cooking water. Peel the chestnuts while still hot and remove the inner skin. Break each into 2 or 3 pieces.

PREPARATION OF DRIED CHESTNUTS:

Soak the dried chestnuts overnight in plenty of cold water. Bring the soaking water and chestnuts to a boil, lower the heat, cover, and simmer for 1 to 1½ hours or until soft (depending on the dryness of the chestnuts it may take as long as 2 hours). Reserve ½ cup of the cooking water. Break each chestnut into 2 or 3 pieces.

CHICKEN COOKED IN SANGIOVESE WINE

Pollo al Vino Sangiovese

4 to 6 servings

- 1 2-to-3-pound chicken, cut into serving pieces, dried
- ¾ cup all-purpose flour
- 2 tablespoons olive oil
- 2 tablespoons butter
- *battuto*: 1 onion 1 carrot, 1 stalk celery, chopped together
- 1 bay leaf
- salt and pepper to taste
- 1 cup Sangiovese wine
- 16 ounces peeled tomatoes, fresh or canned
- 1 cup beef or chicken broth (pages 65, 66)

Coat the chicken pieces with flour. Heat the oil and butter in a heavy-bottomed pot or Dutch oven, brown the chicken pieces, and set aside.

Add the *battuto* to the pot and cook, stirring, until they begin to color. Add the bay leaf and the chicken and some salt and pepper and cook for a few minutes, turning often to blend the flavors. Add the wine and reduce by half. Add the tomatoes and broth. Bring back to a boil, lower the heat, cover and simmer for 50 to 60 minutes or until the chicken is tender. Remove the bay leaf before serving.

TURKEY BREAST WITH TUNA SAUCE

Tacchino Tonnato

4 to 6 servings or up to 12 servings as part of a buffet

This is a classic and very popular do-ahead summer dish that was traditionally made with boiled or roast veal, but is equally delicious made with chicken or turkey breast.

½ of a baked turkey breast, thinly sliced; *or* leftover *bollito* (page 96), veal, chicken, or turkey breast, thinly sliced

TUNA SAUCE:

6-ounce can tuna packed in olive oil

4 anchovy fillets

1 tablespoon salted capers, rinsed

½ cup extra virgin olive oil

¼ cup freshly squeezed lemon juice

Process or blend all the sauce ingredients. The sauce should be as thick as heavy cream and should coat a spoon. If it's too thick, add up to ¼ cup of broth or white wine and blend.

Place the meat slices on a platter in a single layer and spoon the sauce to cover each slice completely. Refrigerate until ready to serve.

FRIED TROUT
Trota Fritta

4 servings

In Emilia-Romagna the trout would be cleaned of its innards, scaled, washed and dried but left whole. If you prefer, have the fish monger remove the heads and fillet.

4 whole trout

1 cup all-purpose flour, seasoned with salt and pepper

4 tablespoons olive oil

4 tablespoons butter

1 lemon, cut into 4 wedges

Coat the fish with the seasoned flour and set aside.

Heat the oil and butter in a frying pan large enough to hold the four fish. Place the fish in the hot pan and fry until crisp and golden. Turn to cook the other side until crisp. Serve hot with a squeeze of lemon juice.

DRIED CODFISH FRITTERS
Frittelline di Baccala

4 to 6 servings

- 8 ounces *baccala* (dried codfish), soaked overnight
- 1½ cups milk
- 1½ cups all-purpose flour
- 1 teaspoon baking powder
- ½ cup canola oil for frying

Flake the codfish and set aside.

Mix the milk, flour, and baking powder into a smooth batter. Add the codfish, stir and let stand while you heat the oil in a large frying pan. Make the fritters by dropping one tablespoon of the fish mixture for each fritter into the hot oil. Cook fritters on both sides until delicately browned. As the fritters cook, place them on paper towels to remove the residual oil.

Serve hot or at room temperature as a snack with a glass of wine, as part of an antipasto, or as part of a meal with a salad.

CLASSIC FISH STEW OF ROMAGNA

Brodetto

6 to 8 servings

***Brodetto** was traditionally prepared by fishermen with sea water and the catch of the day, but more often than not with the fish that they couldn't sell. It's best when made with a variety of fish flavored with wine, tomato purée, olive oil, onions, and just a touch of vinegar. The whole fish is used, with the heads and carcasses leftover after filleting each fish used to make a rich broth and the fillets served in the **brodetto**.*

4 pounds whole fish, such as red snapper, white fish, flounder, sea bass, cod, or sea trout

½ pound shrimp

1 pound squid

1 pound small clams

½ cup extra virgin olive oil

2 onions, chopped

½ cup red wine vinegar

1 cup white wine

8 cups prepared fish broth

salt and pepper to taste

2 loaves of Italian bread, sliced and toasted or grilled

BROTH:

¼ cup extra virgin olive oil

2 cloves garlic, sliced

8 sprigs Italian flat-leaf parsley with stems

Preparation of seafood:
Clean and fillet the whole fish (or ask the fishmonger to do it for you). Set aside the heads and bones to make the broth. Wash and shell the shrimp and set aside the shells for the broth. Wash the squid, remove and discard the eyes and bone, cut the body into rings and leave the tentacles whole and set aside. Scrub and wash the clams and set aside.

Preparation of broth:
Heat the olive oil in a large pot and cook the garlic until it barely begins to color. Add the parsley, lemon zest, and tomato puree and bring to a boil. Add the fish heads and bones, shrimp shells, salt, and peppercorns and cook for 5 minutes. Add 8 cups of cold water, return to a boil, lower the heat, cover, and simmer for 40 minutes. Cool, strain, discard the solids, and refrigerate until ready to use. (Yields about 8 cups.)

- 2 strips fresh lemon zest
- 16 ounces tomato puree
- Fish heads, fish bones, and shrimp shells, washed
- 1 teaspoon salt
- 1 teaspoon whole peppercorns

Preparation of stew:
Heat the oil in a large pot, add the onions, stir and cook until soft and fragrant. Add the vinegar and continue stirring until the vinegar is reduced. Add the wine and stir and cook with the onions for 5 minutes. Add the reserved fish broth and bring to a boil. Add the squid, simmer gently for 20 minutes. Add salt and pepper to taste. Add the fish fillets and cook 10 minutes. Add the shrimp and clams and simmer 5 minutes until the clams open. Turn off the heat.

Serve the *brodetto* in large bowls over one or two slices of toasted or grilled Italian bread, making sure that each serving includes a variety of fish and seafood and plenty of the flavorful broth.

SAUCES
Salse

SALSE
SAUCES

GREEN SAUCE

Salsa Verde

Juice the lemons with a reamer, keeping the four lemon halves intact, and use them to serve the green sauce elegantly in these natural "bowls." Be sure to cut a thin slice off the tops and bottoms of the lemons so that the lemon bowls stand straight on the serving platter when filled.

bunch of Italian flat-leaf parsley
6 anchovy fillets
½ onion, chopped
¼ cup salted capers, rinsed
juice of 2 lemons
¾ cup extra virgin olive oil

Remove the tough stems from the parsley, wash and spin dry. Chop the parsley leaves in a food processor, add the anchovies, onion, capers, and lemon juice. Immediately begin to add the olive oil, pulsing until you reach the desired consistency. Serve with *bollito misto* (page 96), fish, or vegetables.

RED SAUCE

Salsa Rossa

¼ cup extra virgin olive oil
1 onion, chopped
1½ pounds tomatoes, blanched, peeled, and chopped
5 sprigs basil, chopped
1 teaspoon sugar
salt and pepper to taste

Heat the olive oil in a medium saucepan. Add the onion and cook until soft. Add the tomatoes, basil, sugar, salt, and pepper. Bring to a boil, lower the heat, and simmer for 30 minutes, giving the sauce an occasional stir. Serve with *bollito misto* (page 96) or on *tagliatelle* (page 35) topped with freshly grated Parmigiano-Reggiano cheese.

MAYONNAISE
Salsa Maionese

2 egg yolks
½ teaspoon salt
2 teaspoons lemon juice
1 cup extra virgin olive oil or other vegetable oil

Whisk the egg yolks until light. Add the salt and one teaspoon of the lemon juice, and continue whisking. Begin to add the olive oil a few drops at a time until it begins to emulsify, then add the other teaspoon of lemon juice and the remainder of the oil in a very fine stream until the mayonnaise is thick and smooth.

BLENDER MAYONNAISE
Salsa Maionese Frullata

This is a lighter version that uses the whole egg instead of 2 egg yolks.

1 egg
½ teaspoon salt
1 cup olive oil or other vegetable oil
1 tablespoon lemon juice

Place the egg in the blender container and turn on high. While blending, add the salt and half of the oil in a very fine stream until it begins to emulsify. Continue blending as you add the lemon juice and the remainder of the oil.

BÉCHAMEL SAUCE (WHITE SAUCE)

Salsa Besciamella

Besciamella ***is one of the basic ingredients of Lasagne Bolognese (page 46) that enriches and adds to the silken mouth feel of this delicious traditional dish.***

¼ cup butter
¼ cup all-purpose flour
2 cups milk, scalded
salt and pepper to taste
dash of freshly grated nutmeg

Heat the butter in a medium saucepan, add the flour and stir to blend. Slowly add the milk whisking to blend and remove lumps. Stir over medium heat until the sauce boils and is thick and velvety. Add salt and pepper to taste and the nutmeg.

LOW-FAT BÉCHAMEL SAUCE

Salsa Besciamella Magra

It is the smoothness of béchamel sauce that makes it delicious, not its fat content, so it's equally good made with low fat milk and without the usual butter.

2 cups warm 1% or 2% milk
¼ cup all-purpose flour
salt and pepper to taste
dash of freshly grated nutmeg

Place ½ cup of the milk and the flour in a jar with a tight fitting screw top. Shake vigorously to mix. Meanwhile, heat the rest of the milk with the salt, pepper, and nutmeg. Whisk in the flour mixture and continue to cook and stir until it comes to a boil and the sauce is thick and velvety.

CLASSIC BOLOGNESE SAUCE

Classico Ragù Bolognese

Makes 1½ quarts (6 cups)

This is a classic meat sauce created by slow cooking using wine and a rich meat broth that are allowed to reduce to develop a more complex flavor. In the second Bolognese sauce recipe (opposite page), the tomato flavor is more assertive, but both sauces are enriched with the addition of heavy cream at the end of the cooking time.

4 tablespoons butter

4 tablespoons extra virgin olive oil

battuto: 1 onion, 1 carrot, 1 stalk celery, finely chopped together

1½ pounds ground beef, veal, and pork in any combination

1 cup white wine

1 tablespoon Italian tomato paste

4 cups homemade meat broth (page 65)

salt and pepper to taste

1 cup heavy cream

Heat the butter and oil in a large saucepan. Add the *battuto* and cook until soft. Add the meat and brown, stirring to separate. Add the wine, stir and cook until it reduces by half.

Make a hot spot in the pan by pushing the meat to the side. Add the tomato paste, stir and cook for a minute, then add 2 cups of the broth and stir all together. Add salt and pepper to taste, lower the heat, cover and simmer for 2 hours. During cooking be sure to stir from time to time, and add additional broth ½ cup at a time as the liquid concentrates.

Turn off the heat, add the cream and stir. Use some of the sauce fresh and freeze the remainder in pint containers. One pint is enough for 1 pound of pasta or noodles.

BOLOGNESE SAUCE
Ragù Bolognese

Makes 2 quarts (8 cups)

- 2 tablespoons butter
- 2 tablespoons extra virgin olive oil
- 2 ounces pancetta, cubed
- *battuto*: 1 onion, 1 carrot, 1 stalk celery, finely chopped together
- 2 pounds ground beef, veal, and pork in any combination
- 1 cup white wine
- 2 (28 ounce) cans Italian plum tomatoes, pureed
- salt and pepper to taste
- 1 cup heavy cream

Heat the butter and oil in a large saucepan. Add the pancetta and when it begins to brown add the *battuto* and cook until soft. Add the meat and stir to separate. Add the wine and stir and cook until it reduces by half.

Add the pureed tomatoes and one can of water. Add salt and pepper to taste, lower the heat, cover and simmer for 2 hours.

Use some of the sauce fresh and freeze the remainder in pint containers. One pint is enough for 1 pound of pasta or noodles.

PROSCIUTTO SAUCE

Salsa al Prosciutto

6 to 8 servings

- 8 tablespoons butter
- 2 onions, chopped
- 1 bay leaf
- 8 ounces sliced prosciutto, chopped
- ¾ cup white wine
- ½ cup (2 ounces) grated Parmigiano-Reggiano cheese

Heat the butter in a medium saucepan. Add the onions and bay leaf and allow the onion to soften but not brown. Add the chopped prosciutto and stir to mix. Add the wine and continue to stir until it reduces by half. Add the grated cheese, stir and turn off the heat. Remove the bay leaf. Taste and adjust the salt (since the prosciutto is already salty additional salt may not be necessary).

Serve this sauce on cooked fresh *tagliatelle* noodles (page 35), other pasta, or gnocchi, adding a ladle of the pasta cooking water to the sauce if it seems too dry. Top with additional freshly grated Parmigiano-Reggiano cheese, toss lightly and serve.

MUSHROOM SAUCE
Salsa al Funghi

6 to 8 servings

- 8 tablespoons butter
- 4 ounces pancetta, chopped
- 4 scallions, sliced into rounds
- 4 sprigs fresh Italian flat-leaf parsley, chopped
- 2 pounds fresh mixed mushrooms, such as white, cremini, oyster, shitake, portobello, sliced
- ½ cup white wine
- 1 cup chicken broth (page 66)
- salt and black pepper to taste

Heat 4 tablespoons of the butter in a medium saucepan. Add the pancetta and cook until crisp. Add the scallions, stir, and cook for a few minutes until they soften. Stir in the parsley and add the mushrooms. Add the wine and cook while stirring to reduce the pan liquid by half.

Add the broth and some salt and pepper to taste, lower the heat, cover, and simmer, stirring occasionally, for 20 minutes. If it looks too dry, add ¼ cup of boiling water during cooking or a ladle of pasta cooking water at the end.

Turn off the heat, add the rest of the butter and stir to melt the butter and thicken the sauce. Serve over hot *tagliatelle* (page 35), other pasta, or polenta (page 87).

MARJORAM SAUCE FROM ROMAGNA

Salsa Romagnola alla Maggiorana

Makes about 4 cups

- 4 tablespoons butter
- *battuto*: 1 onion, 1 carrot, finely chopped together
- 1 bay leaf
- 1 pound Italian sausage with casings removed
- 1 28-ounce can Italian plum tomatoes, pureed
- 1 cup beef or chicken broth (pages 65, 66
- salt and pepper to taste
- 5 sprigs fresh marjoram, leaves taken off the stems and chopped

Heat the butter in a medium saucepan. Add the *battuto* and bay leaf and cook until fragrant. Add the sausage and stir until brown. Add the tomato puree, broth, and salt and pepper, bring to a boil, lower the heat, and simmer for 45 minutes or until thickened. Add the marjoram, stir, and remove from the heat. Serve on rigatoni, penne, or fresh *garganelli* (page 40).

SIDE DISHES AND SALADS

Contorni e Insalate

CONTORNI E INSALATE
SIDE DISHES AND SALADS

ONIONS COOKED IN TREBBIANO WINE

Cipolline al Trebbiano

6 to 8 servings

2 pounds white onions
½ cup extra virgin olive oil
1 cup Trebbiano wine
1 bay leaf
½ teaspoon salt
2 sprigs fresh rosemary

Drop the unpeeled onions in boiling water, cook for 2 minutes. Drain, immerse onions in cold water, peel, and set aside.

Place the olive oil, wine, bay leaf, and salt in a chef's pan and bring to a boil. Add the peeled onions, bring back to a boil, add the rosemary, lower the heat and simmer for 20 to 30 minutes or until cooked through.

SPINACH WITH PARMIGIANO

Spinaci Conditi

4 to 6 servings

2 10-ounce packages fresh spinach
salt to taste
a fresh grating of nutmeg
6 tablespoons butter, divided
¾ cup (3 ounces) freshly grated Parmigiano-Reggiano cheese

Soak the spinach in cold water for 15 minutes. Take off the tough stems and wash the leaves in several changes of water, but don't spin dry. Place the wet spinach in a large pot, sprinkle with salt and the nutmeg, cover and heat. Allow to wilt for 6 to 8 minutes turning several times with tongs.

Keeping the cover loosely on the pot, drain out the cooking liquid, and add half of the butter and ½ cup of the grated Parmigiano-Reggiano. Turn with the tongs to mix and cook for 2 minutes so that the spinach absorbs the butter and cheese. Spoon the cooked spinach into a serving dish. Dot with the remaining butter and a *nevicata* or "snowfall" (about ¼ cup) of freshly grated Parmigiano-Reggiano cheese before bringing to the table.

ASPARAGUS PARMA-STYLE

Asparagi alla Parmigiana

6 to 8 servings

- 2 pounds fresh asparagus
- 4 tablespoons butter
- ½ cup (2 ounces) freshly grated Parmigiano-Reggiano cheese

Preheat oven to 375 degrees. Snap the ends off the asparagus and reserve for soup. Wash the tips, place in a baking pan, cover with 1 inch of boiling water and let stand for 10 minutes. Drain the asparagus, place in a baking pan that you can bring to the table, dot with butter, top with a *nevicata* or "snowfall" of Parmigiano-Reggiano cheese, and bake in the preheated 375-degree oven for 15 to 20 minutes or until the asparagus is tender, the butter melts, and the cheese forms a light crust. Serve hot.

AUNT ELVIRA'S PEAS

Piselliini di Zia Elvira

6 to 8 servings

Frozen tiny tender peas are available all year, and since they are packaged very young before they develop the starch of mature peas, they are sugar sweet and much better than even fresh shelled peas. Our beloved Zia Elvira made this recipe often to the delight of the whole family.

- 4 tablespoons butter
- 4 tablespoons extra virgin olive oil
- 1 small onion, chopped
- 2 10-ounce packages frozen tender tiny peas
- salt and pepper to taste

Heat the butter and oil in a medium saucepan, add the onion and cook until softened but not browned. Add the peas, salt and pepper to taste, and 2 tablespoons of water. Lower the heat, cover and cook for 7 to 10 minutes. Serve hot or at room temperature.

PEAS AND ARTICHOKES

Piselli e Carciofi

4 to 6 servings

- 8 baby artichokes
- 2 tablespoons butter
- 2 tablespoons olive oil
- 1 clove garlic, chopped
- 2 tablespoons Italian flat-leaf parsley, chopped
- salt and pepper to taste
- 1 10-ounce package frozen tender tiny peas

To prepare the artichokes: Remove the outer leaves of the artichokes, trim the stems, cut off the tops, and quarter each. Baby artichokes usually don't have a choke, but remove it if necessary. Wash, cut each quarter into 3 slices and place in a bowl of acidulated water (water in which you've squeezed half a lemon) so that they don't darken. Leave the artichokes in the water until ready to cook.

Heat the butter and oil in a medium saucepan or skillet. Add the garlic and when it barely begins to color add the parsley and stir. Add the drained artichokes, ¼ cup water, salt and pepper to taste. Lower the heat, cover and simmer for 15 minutes, or until tender.

Add the frozen peas, stir, cover and cook 5 more minutes, until the peas are just defrosted and heated through.

PEPPERS FROM BERCETO

Peperonata Bercetese

Our friend Annamaria Clerici, lovingly known as "Grande," makes the best **peperonata** ***that is sweet, delicious, light on your stomach, and not only a great antipasto and a great topping for crostini or bruschetta but a wonderful relish, which on this side of the Atlantic is a delicious addition to sandwiches, hamburgers, and even hot dogs.***

- ½ cup extra virgin olive oil
- 1 onion, sliced
- 2 tablespoons Italian tomato concentrate or tomato paste
- 4 red or green bell peppers, seeded, cored, and sliced
- salt to taste

Heat the olive oil in a chef's pan (a low wide pan). Add the sliced onions and stir-fry to soften but not brown. Make a hot spot in the pan by pushing the onions to the sides of the pan and add the tomato paste and stir and cook for 1 minute. Add the peppers and some salt so that they release their liquid. Stir everything together, lower the heat to a bare simmer, cover, and cook for 30 minutes, stirring the *peperonata* once or twice during the cooking time.

Remove the cover and continue to cook, stirring from time to time for another 15 minutes, or until the peppers are tender and fragrant and most of the liquid has been absorbed.

Serve peppers at room temperature.

ROSEMARY ROASTED POTATOES
Patate Arrosto allo Rosmarino

4 to 6 servings

- ½ cup vegetable oil
- 6 potatoes, parboiled, peeled, and sliced
- salt and pepper to taste
- 1 teaspoon fresh chopped rosemary

Preheat the oven to 400 degrees. Place the oil in a baking pan and heat in the oven for 10 minutes. Add the sliced potatoes, sprinkle with salt, pepper, and rosemary, mix to combine, and bake for 30 to 40 minutes until crisp and golden, stirring twice during the baking time.

BAKED FENNEL
Finocchio al Forno

6 to 8 servings

- 2 fennel bulbs, each sliced through the core into 8 wedges
- 4 tablespoons butter
- ½ cup (2 ounces) freshly grated Parmigiano-Reggiano cheese

Preheat oven to 375 degrees. Blanch the fennel in boiling water for 5 minutes. Strain and place in a buttered Pyrex baking dish. Dot with butter and top with grated Parmigiano-Reggiano cheese. Bake in the preheated 375-degree oven for 20 to 30 minutes or until a delicate crust forms on the fennel slices.

BRAISED CABBAGE
Verze Brasate

6 to 8 servings

4 tablespoons butter
2 tablespoons olive oil
1 onion, chopped
4 ounces Italian pancetta, thickly cut and cubed
½ head Savoy cabbage, chopped
½ cup broth or water
salt and pepper to taste

Heat 2 tablespoons butter and the olive oil in a large skillet. Add the onion and pancetta and cook until the onion is softened and the pancetta begins to brown. Add the chopped cabbage and broth or water and stir. Add salt and pepper to taste, cover, lower the heat and simmer for 30 to 40 minutes or until tender. Add the remaining 2 tablespoons of butter and serve hot or at room temperature.

CELERY AND GORGONZOLA SALAD
Insalata di Sedano e Gorgonzola

4 to 6 servings

1 bunch celery
4 ounces gorgonzola cheese
salt and pepper
4 tablespoons olive oil
2 tablespoons white balsamic vinegar

Slice the tender stalks of a bunch of celery, together with some of the inner leaves and place in bowl. Crumble the gorgonzola on top of the celery. Sprinkle with salt and pepper to taste, drizzle with olive oil and white balsamic vinegar and toss. Spoon onto a serving platter and let stand until ready to serve.

POTATO, BEET, AND PEA SALAD
Insalata di Patate, Barbabietole e Piselli

4 to 6 servings

- 2 potatoes, boiled, peeled, and cubed (½ inch)
- 4 beets, boiled or baked, peeled and cubed (½ inch)
- 1 10-ounce package frozen tender tiny peas, defrosted
- salt and pepper to taste
- ¼ cup extra virgin olive oil
- 2 tablespoons balsamic vinegar

Place the potatoes and beets in a bowl. Add the peas, salt and pepper to taste. Drizzle with the olive oil and balsamic vinegar, mix and spoon into a serving dish.

POTATO SALAD
Insalata di Patate

4 to 6 servings

- 6 potatoes, boiled in their jackets, cooled, peeled, and sliced
- salt and pepper to taste
- ⅓ cup extra virgin olive oil
- 2 tablespoons white balsamic vinegar

Place the potato slices in a bowl. Salt and pepper to taste and drizzle with extra virgin olive oil and white balsamic vinegar. Toss and transfer to a serving platter.

WATERCRESS AND ROMAINE SALAD WITH WALNUTS AND PARMIGIANO

Crescione e Lattuga con Noci e Parmigiano

4 to 6 servings

1 bunch watercress
1 head romaine lettuce (just tender leaves)
salt and pepper to taste
¼ cup extra virgin olive oil
2 tablespoons balsamic vinegar
1 cup walnut pieces
shavings of Parmigiano-Reggiano cheese

Remove the tough stems from the watercress, wash, spin dry, and set aside.

Select the tender leaves from the head of romaine lettuce; wash, spin dry, and chop.

Place the greens in a deep bowl, add salt and pepper to taste, drizzle with oil and vinegar, and toss.

Transfer salad to a serving platter, scatter the walnuts on top, and top with Parmigiano-Reggiano shavings. Bring to the table and toss again before serving.

SWEETS
Dolci

Although the preferred end of a meal is cheese and fruit in Italy, wonderful desserts are served at dinner parties or *fuori pasto*, that is to say outside of meals, perhaps with coffee after dinner, with a glass of sweet wine in the afternoon, or on Sunday when visitors are welcomed and entertained. This, of course, puts a spotlight on the wonderful desserts of the region. The *Torta Ferrarese*, particularly the version from Modena that is flavored with chocolate, are unique to Emilia-Romagna in that they are made with the glorious fresh egg noodles for which the region is justly famous. The freshly made super-thin uncooked noodles are layered with sweet fillings, drizzled with plenty of butter, and baked until the top layer turns delicately golden and pleasantly crunchy.

The *crostate,* traditionally made with the fragrant and flavorful fruits and jams of the region, are enjoyed as a *merenda* or afternoon snack, at midmorning with a cup of espresso, or anytime one needs a treat. Our daughter Nicoletta still remembers the magnificent *crostate* that would magically appear as soon as we arrived in Berceto at Grande's house. Grande means big or great, and our friend Annamaria Clerici got her name when her niece, also named Annamaria, was born and she was distinguished as "la Grande" or the big one. As one of the great home cooks of Berceto, she has earned her nickname on both counts.

Then there are the plump, sweet, and flavorful chestnuts, served roasted and piping hot at the end of a festive meal. Friends and family continue to indulge in spirited conversation while shelling them, knowing that. as the proverb says, *"A Tavola Non S'Invecchia,"* which means "At the table one doesn't grow old."

Cordials are offered after dinner and with desserts. Some were traditionally made at home, and we still remember the wonderful *Nocino* that was made by our friend Rino Cagna with 29 (it had to be an odd number) walnuts picked still green on June 24th, the feast of Saint John the Baptist, and macerated in a glass jug in 90 proof alcohol to which a syrup made with spring water and sugar was added along with white wine, cloves, cinnamon, coriander, mace, and lemon peel. The well-corked jug was then placed in a sunny location and turned daily for 40 days before the contents were filtered and bottled. The *Nocino* was allowed to mellow for 2 months before it was enjoyed as a *digestivo* or as a flavorful cordial.

For many years our friends Carlo and Mary Alfare, whose grandparents came from Emilia-Romagna, also made their cordials and gave them as very welcome Christmas gifts. Their specialty was *Liquore di Lamponi*, a raspberry liqueur; they made theirs with homegrown New Jersey raspberries that were macerated in alcohol and sugar syrup until they gave up their beautiful red color and intense fruit flavor to the finished cordial. Today, of course, traditional liquors are purchased in any good wine shop so that they can be enjoyed anytime.

DOLCI
SWEETS

RICE TART
Torta di Riso

6 to 8 servings

4 cups milk

½ cup sugar

pinch of salt

1 teaspoon vanilla extract

grated rind of 1 lemon, divided

1¼ cups arborio rice

26 (5 ounces) Amaretti di Saronno cookies, processed into crumbs

2 tablespoons rum

4 eggs

2 tablespoons butter

2 tablespoons fine dry breadcrumbs

Mix the milk, sugar, salt, vanilla, and half of the grated lemon rind in a saucepan. Add the rice, bring to a boil, lower the flame, cover leaving the cover slightly ajar, and keep at a bare simmer for 20 minutes.

Turn the heat off and while the rice is still hot, stir in the amaretti and let cool, stirring the mixture from time to time. Add the rum, remaining grated lemon rind, 2 of the eggs, and 2 egg yolks. Mix and set aside.

Preheat oven to 350 degrees. Beat the 2 egg whites into a stiff meringue. Butter the bottom and sides of a 9-inch or 10-inch springform pan and lightly coat with breadcrumbs, shaking out the excess crumbs. Fold the meringue into the rice mixture and spoon into the prepared pan.

Bake in the preheated 350-degree oven for 30 to 40 minutes or until lightly golden on top. Cool on a wire rack and unmold when ready to serve.

FRESH NOODLE TART FROM FERRARA

Torta Ferrarese

8 to 12 servings

This simple version of the famous Torta Ferrarese *was once made for my birthday by my cousin Vana Muccio, who was herself a native of Ferrara. This unusual confection is prepared with freshly made uncooked egg noodles that are layered with almonds and sugar and dotted with butter before being baked. Vana made, rolled, and cut the noodles by hand and refused to give me the recipe because she suspected that I would use my Braun kitchen machine noodle attachment that her daughter Luisella had given me as a gift to make them. This is the classic recipe.*

1 tablespoon all-purpose flour

1 tablespoon sugar

8 tablespoons melted butter

SWEET FLAKY PASTRY *PASTA FROLLA DOLCE*:

1½ cups all-purpose flour

½ cup sugar

½ teaspoon salt

4 tablespoons butter

2 egg yolks

grated zest of 1 lemon

2 to 4 tablespoons white wine

EGG NOODLES:

1½ cups all-purpose flour

2 eggs

olive oil

Make the pastry dough: Using your hands or a food processor, mix the flour, sugar, and salt. Cut the butter into the flour mixture. Add the egg yolks and lemon zest and enough wine to make a soft dough. Roll it out into a circle large enough to line a 9-inch or 10-inch springform pan. Line the pan with the pastry and trim the pastry crust even with the top of the pan and set aside.

Make the egg noodles: Using your hands or a food processor, mix the flour and eggs until they form a mass, adding either additional flour or water one tablespoon at a time until you have a rather stiff dough. Shape into a ball, coat with a few drops of olive oil, cover with an inverted bowl and let rest at least 30 minutes. Divide dough in half and roll out each piece by hand on a floured surface until paper thin (or use a pasta machine). When both pieces of dough are rolled out, flour the surfaces

SIMPLE FILLING:

12 ounces whole almonds (2 cups)

¾ cup sugar

TRADITIONAL FILLING:

9 ounces whole almonds (1½ cups)

¾ cup sugar

16 Amaretti di Saronno cookies, crushed

lightly, roll each into a cylinder and slice into the thinnest possible noodles, or cut them with electric cutters at the finest setting. Toss the noodles gently with a sprinkle of flour to unwind them and place them on a towel covered pan until ready to use.

Make the filling: For the simple filling, process the almonds and sugar into a coarse chop and set aside. For the traditional filling, coarsely chop the almonds and mix with the sugar and the crushed amaretti cookies or pulse the almonds, sugar, and amaretti in a food processor into a coarse chop (be careful not to reduce to a powder).

Preheat oven to 350 degrees.

Assemble the cake: Sprinkle the 1 tablespoon flour and 1 tablespoon sugar on the bottom of the pastry-lined springform pan. Take ⅓ of the fresh uncooked noodles and make the first layer. Sprinkle ½ of the filling on the noodles, add another layer of noodles and the rest of the filling. Top with the remaining noodles and drizzle with the melted butter. If the filling doesn't quite reach the top of the pan, fold the pastry crust over the noodles all around. Bake in the preheated 350-degree oven for 30 to 40 minutes or until the top layer of noodles is golden and slightly crispy. Serve warm or at room temperature.

NOTE: The noodles for this recipe must be freshly made, still soft, and each layer of noodles should be about 1-inch thick but not packed down. If one recipe of noodles proves to be too much for one cake, freeze the rest or air dry them and keep in a closed container to add to a soup.

CHOCOLATE TART FROM MODENA

Torta alla Cioccolata di Modena

8 to 12 servings

This tart, like torta Ferrarese *(page 146), is made with fresh uncooked egg noodles, but this filling is enriched with chocolate and candied citrus fruit and peels.*

- 1 tablespoon all-purpose flour
- 1 tablespoon sugar
- 8 tablespoons melted butter

SWEET FLAKY PASTRY
PASTA FROLLA DOLCE:

- 1½ cups all-purpose flour
- ½ cup sugar
- ½ teaspoon salt
- 4 tablespoons butter
- 2 egg yolks
- grated zest of 1 lemon
- 2 to 4 tablespoons white wine

EGG NOODLES:

- 1½ cups all-purpose flour
- 2 eggs
- olive oil

Make the pastry dough: Using your hands or a food processor, mix the flour, sugar, and salt. Cut the butter into the flour mixture. Add the egg yolks and lemon zest and enough wine to make a soft dough. Roll it out into a circle large enough to line a 9-inch or 10-inch springform pan. Line the pan with the pastry and trim the pastry crust even with the top of the pan and set aside.

Make the egg noodles: Using your hands or a food processor, mix the flour and eggs until they form a mass, adding either additional flour or water one tablespoon at a time until you have a rather stiff dough. Shape into a ball, coat with a few drops of olive oil, cover with an inverted bowl and let rest at least 30 minutes. Divide dough in half and roll out each piece by hand on a floured surface until paper thin (or use a pasta machine). When both pieces of dough are rolled out, flour the surfaces lightly, roll each into a cylinder and slice into the thinnest possible noodles, or cut them with electric cutters at the finest setting. Toss the noodles gently with a sprinkle of flour to unwind them and place them on a towel covered pan until ready to use.

CHOCOLATE FILLING:

6 ounces (1 cup) whole almonds

¾ cup sugar

4 ounces semisweet chocolate

4 ounces (½ cup) candied citron, lemon peel, and/or orange peel in any combination

Make the filling: Coarsely chop the almonds, either by hand or in a food processor and add the sugar. Place in a bowl. Coarsely chop the chocolate and add to the almond and sugar mixture. Chop the candied fruit coarsely, preferably by hand, and add to the mixture. (Don't over process any of the ingredients as it will reduce the filling to a paste; the ingredients should be just coarsely chopped by pulsing a few times if done in a processor.)

Preheat oven to 350 degrees.

Assemble the cake: Sprinkle the 1 tablespoon flour and 1 tablespoon sugar on the bottom of the pastry-lined pan. Take ⅓ of the fresh uncooked noodles and make the first layer. Sprinkle ½ of the filling on the noodles, add another layer of noodles and the rest of the filling. Top with the remaining noodles and drizzle with the melted butter. If the filling doesn't quite reach the top of the pan, fold the edge of the pastry crust over the noodles all around. Bake in the preheated 350-degree oven for 30 to 40 minutes or until the top layer of noodles is golden and slightly crispy. Serve warm or at room temperature.

NOTE: The noodles for this recipe must be freshly made, still soft, and each layer of noodles should be about 1-inch thick but not packed down. If one recipe of noodles proves to be too much for one cake, freeze the rest or air dry them and keep in a closed container to add to a soup.

PLUM TART
Crostata di Susine

6 to 8 servings

Our daughter Nicoletta thought that it was by magic that our friend Annamaria always had a Crostata di Susine *ready whenever we arrived in Berceto.*

FLAKY DOUGH FOR TARTS
PASTA FROLLA PER CROSTATE:

8 tablespoons butter

2½ cups all-purpose flour

2 tablespoons sugar

½ teaspoon salt

2 egg yolks

grated zest of 1 lemon

1 to 2 tablespoons ice water, if needed

beaten egg for glazing lattice strips

PLUM FILLING:

10 Amaretti di Saronno cookies

¼ cup rum or vermouth

12-ounce jar plum jam

Preheat the oven to 350 degrees. Cut the butter into the flour, add the sugar, salt, egg yolks, and water, if necessary, adding 1 tablespoon at a time until you have a workable dough. Set aside ⅓ of the dough. Shape the rest of the dough into a ball, roll out into a circle and fit into a 10-inch tart or quiche pan allowing the dough to overhang the edge of the pan by 1 inch.

Coarsely crush the amaretti, drizzle with the rum or vermouth and let stand until the liquid is absorbed. Distribute the soaked amaretti on top of the crust. Spread the jam on top of the amaretti.

Roll out the small piece of dough. Brush with egg glaze. Cut into ½-inch strips with a fluted pastry wheel. Place one strip in the middle of the tart and 3 on either side. Place the same number at an angle to the first set on the top of the *crostata* to form a lattice design. Fold the overhanging edge of the dough over the filling. Place the tart in the preheated 350-degree oven and bake for 30 to 40 minutes. Remove from the oven and cool to room temperature.

APRICOT TART
Crostata di Albicocche

For an equally delicious variation, follow the above recipe substituting apricot jam for the plum jam and marsala wine for the rum or vermouth.

ALMOND TART
Crostata di Mandorle

6 to 8 servings

Another of our Bercetese friend Annamaria Clerici's specialties was this tender and deliciously fragrant Crostata di Mandorle.

- 1 recipe *pasta frolla per crostate* dough (page 150)
- ¼ cup milk to glaze lattice strips

ALMOND FILLING:

- 16 Amaretti di Saronno cookies, crushed
- 1 cup (6 ounces) almonds, toasted, cooled, and finely chopped but not pulverized
- 4 tablespoons butter, at room temperature
- ¾ cup sugar
- 1 egg
- 1 egg yolk

Preheat oven to 350 degrees.

Mix the amaretti and almonds and set aside. Cream the butter and sugar, add the egg and egg yolk, and mix. Fold in the amaretti and almond mixture and set aside.

Remove ⅓ of the *pasta frolla* dough and set aside. Shape the rest into a ball, roll out into a circle, and fit into a 10-inch tart or quiche pan, allowing the dough to overhang the edge of the pan by one inch. Roll out the other piece of dough into a rectangle, brush with milk, cut into strips with a fluted pastry wheel, and set aside.

Spoon the filling into the crust, arrange the strips in a lattice design, fold the overhanging edge over the filling. Bake in the preheated 350-degree oven for 40 to 50 minutes.

WHITE ALMOND CAKE

Torta Bianca di Mandorle

8 to 10 servings

This was the favorite cake of our friend Irene Berni who treated us to this delightful white cake each time we visited her in Bardi. Villa Berni is located in the main square of the town within walking distance of the castle of Bardi which her grandchildren Carl, Anthony, and Marisa Berni and their mother Laura immortalized in a beautiful handpainted panel on Da Vinci's Dream, the wave swinger ride that is one of the most popular at Canobie Lake Amusement Park in Salem, New Hampshire, and in which the Berni Family is a partner.

- 1½ cups blanched almonds
- 3 eggs, separated
- 1½ cups sugar
- 2 sticks (8 ounces) butter, melted
- 2 cups all-purpose flour
- 1 teaspoon baking powder
- 2 tablespoons rum

Preheat the oven to 375 degrees. Butter a tube pan well. Grind the almonds into a fine meal in a food processor and set aside.

Beat the egg whites into a meringue with ¾ cup of the sugar.

Without washing the beaters, in another bowl beat the yolks with the remaining ¾ cup sugar. Add the melted butter to the beaten yolks and fold in the ground almonds, flour, and baking powder, alternating with half of the meringue and the rum. Fold in the remainder of the meringue.

Spoon batter into the well-buttered tube pan and bake at 375 degrees for 40 minutes. Allow to cool, unmold, and dust with confectioner's sugar.

FRESH FRUIT TART

Crostata di Frutta Fresca

6 to 8 servings

1 recipe *pasta frolla per crostate* dough (page 150)

LEMON PASTRY CREAM *CREMA PASTICCERA AL LIMONE*:

¼ cup cornstarch

2 cups milk

⅔ cup sugar

2 egg yolks

strip of lemon peel

FRUIT TOPPING:

strawberries, blueberries, raspberries, sliced peaches, sliced kiwi, and/or seedless grapes

a few sprigs of mint, if available

½ cup clear apple jelly, heated until melted

Preheat the oven to 350 degrees.

For the pastry cream: Place the cornstarch in a jar with a tight-fitting lid, add ½ cup of milk and shake vigorously until well-blended with no lumps. Pour the remaining 1½ cups milk in a small saucepan and whisk in the sugar and egg yolks until well mixed. Add the cornstarch mixture as well as the lemon peel. Place over medium heat and stir with a wooden spoon until it comes to a boil and thickens. Remove and discard the piece of lemon peel. Place a piece of buttered wax or parchment paper on the surface of the *crema* to avoid the formation of a film and cool while you bake the crust.

Roll out the dough to fit into a 9-inch tart pan, trim the edges even with the top of the pan, prick the bottom with a fork, and bake in the preheated 350-degree oven for 20 to 30 minutes. Remove from the oven and cool on a rack.

Spoon the lemon cream into the crust and top with fruit in season in a decorative pattern. (Concentric circles of fruit in contrasting colors or the same fruit overlapped in different directions both work well.) Brush the fruit with hot apple jelly, decorate with sprigs of mint and refrigerate tart until ready to serve.

CHRISTMAS FRUIT CAKE
Spongata

8 to 12 servings

Spongata is one of the oldest Italian desserts, going back to medieval times and some say to Roman times. During one of our summer visits to Berceto, a local filmmaker showed a very interesting documentary on the making of this traditional cake, from the gathering of nuts and fruits, each in its own season, through the drying, roasting, preserving, and candying of the various elements, to the final assembly of a holiday cake that was proudly given as a gift. The film was shown in the piazza. People came with their chairs to see it on a large screen that had been set up for the occasion, and we saw it from the balcony. There is an historic document which attests to the fact that a spongata was sent to the Duke Francesco Sforza of Milano in 1454. It was the favorite cake of Giuseppe Verdi, and one of the commercial brands has a picture of the maestro on its decorative wrapper.

FILLING:

½ cup raisins

1 cup (6 ounces) whole blanched almonds

½ cup sugar

1 cup honey

½ cup fine breadcrumbs made from toasted bread

½ teaspoon cinnamon

½ teaspoon nutmeg

½ teaspoon ground black pepper

½ cup (3 ounces) filberts, blanched, skinned, lightly toasted, and coarsely chopped

½ cup (3 ounces) walnuts, coarsely chopped

Soak the raisins in warm water to cover for 30 minutes, drain and set aside. Coarsely grind the almonds and sugar in a food processor and set aside.

Heat the honey until it liquefies, add the breadcrumbs, almond mixture, cinnamon, nutmeg, and black pepper. Mix well and let cool. Add the filberts, walnuts, pine nuts, candied citron, candied orange peel, salt, and cognac and mix well. Place in a covered container and let rest for at least 24 hours and as long as 2 weeks to develop and combine the flavors.

When ready to make the *spongata*, mix all the ingredients for the dough by hand or in a food processor, knead a few turns, wrap in plastic, and refrigerate until ready to use.

¼ cup pine nuts

½ cup candied citron, finely chopped

¼ cup candied orange peel, finely chopped

pinch of salt

2 tablespoons cognac

DOUGH:

2 cups all-purpose flour

½ cup sugar

½ cup butter

¼ to ½ cup white wine

grated zest of ½ lemon

Preheat the oven to 350 degrees. Divide the dough into 2 pieces, one larger than the other. Shape each into a ball. Roll out the larger ball into a circle that will fit a 10-inch to 12-inch tart pan and overhang by 1 inch. Place the pastry in the tart pan. Fill the tart with the filling. Roll out the second ball of dough to fit the top of the filling, dab a little water along the edge and fold the overhanging dough over the top crust to seal. Using a skewer or a chopstick, make holes all over the top crust. Bake in the 350-degree oven for 20 to 30 minutes. The crust should barely begin to color.

Cool the cake and sprinkle with some powdered sugar. Wrap and place in a tin or a covered container if you're going to keep it for a long time. The *spongata* will keep for 2 to 3 months. This is a rich confection that is served in thin slices.

NOTE: Preparation of this cake needs to start days, weeks, or even months in advance.

TRIFLE DESSERT FROM REGGIO-EMILIA

Zuppa Inglese di Reggio-Emilia

8 to 12 servings

This is a classic Italian dessert with regional variations. It allows Italians to make fun of the venerable English trifle, which is always assembled in a glass bowl, by calling it "English soup." Zuppa Inglese *is layered and molded in a springform pan for a wonderful presentation. The* Pan di Spaga *sponge cake was traditionally moistened with Alchermes, giving the* Zuppa Inglese *its typical red color. Since Alchermes, made with cochineal beetle shells which give it its vibrant crimson color, is not available outside of Italy, and it's hard to find even there, a sugar syrup with the addition of cognac, rum, or one's favorite liqueur is substituted without loss of flavor.*

ITALIAN SPONGE CAKE
PAN DI SPAGNA:

1 cup all-purpose flour

1 teaspoon baking powder

6 eggs, separated

1 cup sugar

1 teaspoon vanilla extract

SUGAR SYRUP:

1½ cups sugar

½ cup cognac, rum, your favorite liqueur, or juice from a jar of maraschino cherries

CHOCOLATE AND VANILLA CREAM
CREMA ALLA VANIGLIA E ALLA CIOCCOLATA:

½ cup cornstarch

4 cups milk

Preheat oven to 350 degrees.

Make the sponge cake: Mix the flour and baking powder and set aside. In one bowl, add ½ cup of the sugar and the vanilla to the egg yolks and set aside. In another bowl, whip the egg whites until stiff, add the remainder of the sugar a little at a time until the meringue stands in firm peaks. Take the beater and without washing it, beat the egg yolk mixture until thick and light yellow. Fold in the flour mixture along with ⅓ of the meringue to lighten up the batter. Fold in the rest of the meringue until it's incorporated. Spread the batter on a greased jelly roll pan, leveling the top with an offset spatula. Bake in the preheated 350-degree oven for 20 to 30 minutes or until the cake is a light golden color. Cool on a wire rack. Cut the cake in half down the middle and then into ½-inch slices.

1⅓ cups sugar
4 egg yolks
2 teaspoons vanilla extract
4 tablespoons cocoa

TOPPINGS:

2 ounces bittersweet chocolate, shaved with a potato peeler; *or* 1 cup heavy cream, whipped

Make the sugar syrup: Mix 1½ cups water and the sugar in a small saucepan. Bring to a boil, lower the heat, and simmer for 5 minutes. Cool, add the liqueur or maraschino juice, pour into a spray bottle and set aside.

Make the cream: Place the cornstarch in a jar with a tight-fitting lid, add 1 cup milk, and shake vigorously until well-blended with no lumps. Pour the remaining 3 cups milk in a small saucepan and whisk in the sugar and egg yolks until well mixed. Add the cornstarch mixture and whisk well. Place over medium heat and stir with a wooden spoon until mixture comes to a boil and thickens. Remove from heat and add the vanilla extract. Pour half of the vanilla cream into a bowl. Add the cocoa to the portion still in the pot, place over low heat and stir until the cocoa is incorporated into the cream.

Assemble the trifle: Line the bottom and sides of a springform pan with thin slices of the sponge cake and spray with ⅓ of the syrup. Spread the chocolate cream on top of sponge cake. Make a second layer of sponge cake, moisten with half of the remaining syrup, spread the vanilla cream on top. Make a third layer of sponge cake, moisten with the rest of the syrup, cover with plastic wrap and refrigerate overnight or for at least 4 hours.

When ready to serve, remove the sides of the springform pan and top the *Zuppa Inglese* with shaved chocolate or whipped cream.

FRIED CHESTNUT-FILLED PASTRIES

Tortelli di Castagne Fritte

Sapa, which is a traditional reduced grape must, has been used as a sweetener since ancient times and is available in Italian grocery stores. Honey can be substituted for sapa. *Mostarda is preserved fruit that has been cooked in grape must (*mosto *– hence the name* mostarda*) and flavored with mustard, which in Italian is called* senape.

DOUGH:

3 cups all-purpose flour

pinch of salt

¼ cup olive oil

½ cup white wine

FILLING:

½ pound prepared chestnuts, either freshly cooked (page 109) or jarred

¼ cup *sapa*

¼ cup toasted almonds, chopped

1 ounce bitter chocolate, chopped

4 ounces *mostarda*, chopped

grated zest of 1 orange

½ teaspoon ground cinnamon

2 tablespoons *nocino* or rum

3 cups vegetable oil for deep frying

½ cup confectioner's sugar for dusting

By hand or in a food processor using pulse mix all the dough ingredients until they form a mass. Place the dough on a counter, knead a few turns, coat with a film of olive oil, cover with an inverted bowl, and let rest for 30 minutes or until ready to use.

Mash the chestnuts with a potato masher or pulse in a food processor leaving them a little bit chunky for texture. Mix in the *sapa*, almonds, chocolate, *mostarda*, orange zest, cinnamon, and rum to make a thick paste.

Roll out the dough not too thin on a well-floured board, or use a pasta machine and roll out the dough to the next to the last setting. Cut dough into 2-inch circles. Place a teaspoon of filling in the center of each piece of dough, fold into a half moon, seal the edges well, and place on a towel until all are made. Gather the scraps into a ball, roll out again and make more pastries.

Heat the oil and deep fry the pastries until golden brown on both sides. Drain on paper towels, cool, dust with confectioner's sugar, and serve. Any leftover scraps of dough can also be fried and sprinkled with powdered sugar.

TRADITIONAL CHESTNUT TART
Castagnaccio

6 to 8 servings

½ cup raisins
2 cups chestnut flour
½ cup sugar
¼ cup extra virgin olive oil
½ cup pine nuts
needles from a sprig of fresh rosemary
Optional: 1 cup heavy cream, whipped

Preheat the oven to 375 degrees. Soak the raisins in 1 cup boiling water for 30 minutes, then drain the soaking water into a measuring cup and add enough additional water to make 2¼ cups.

Mix the soaked raisins, chestnut flour, sugar, half of the olive oil, and 2¼ cups raisin water and pour into a buttered or oiled 10-inch ceramic quiche pan. Drizzle the remaining oil on the batter, sprinkle the pine nuts and rosemary needles on top of the tart. Bake in the preheated 375-degree oven for 40 to 45 minutes or until the top is dry. Serve at room temperature with a spoonful of whipped cream, if desired.

CHESTNUT DESSERT
Dolce di Castagne

6 to 8 servings

- 1 pound prepared chestnuts, either freshly cooked (page 109) or jarred
- ½ cup confectioner's sugar
- 8 ounces mascarpone cheese
- 2 tablespoons liqueur, such as *nocino*, or sweet wine, such as marsala
- 1 cup heavy cream, whipped

Process the chestnuts into a puree. Add the sugar, mascarpone, and liqueur and pulse to mix.

Place an inverted empty glass in the center of a serving platter. Place the chestnut mixture in a potato ricer and let the strands fall onto the platter around the glass. Remove the glass and fill the space with whipped cream.

CANDIED CHESTNUTS
Castagne Caramellate

6 to 8 servings

- ¾ cup sugar
- 1 pound peeled fresh chestnuts; *or* 1 jar unsweetened prepared chestnuts
- ½ teaspoon vanilla extract
- 1 cup heavy cream, whipped

Place 1½ cups water and the sugar in a small pot, bring to a boil and simmer for 5 minutes. Add the chestnuts, bring back to a boil, lower the heat to a slow simmer, cover, and cook for 30 to 40 minutes or until most but not all of the syrup is absorbed. Turn off the heat and add the vanilla. Cool to room temperature and serve the chestnuts moistened with a little of the syrup and a dollop of whipped cream.

STUFFED BAKED PEACHES
Pesche Ripiene al Forno

6 servings

My cousin Vana Muccio, who was a native of Emilia-Romagna, made this delicious dessert often as a favorite summer treat when peaches were in full season. Her daughter Luisella continues the tradition to the delight of her son Manuel, her brother Gianfranco, his wife Chantal, and all of us who enjoy this classic dessert that can always be relied upon to bring back so many pleasant family memories.

6 peaches
3 tablespoons butter
1 cup white wine
½ cup sugar

FILLING:

8 Amaretti di Saronno cookies, crushed
3 tablespoons sugar
⅓ cup (2 ounces) almonds, ground
1 egg yolk
1 to 2 tablespoons Amaretto di Saronno liqueur or your favorite liqueur

Cut the peaches in half, remove the pits, and with a teaspoon or a small melon-baller, scoop out some of the pulp around the pit to enlarge the hole. Place the peach pulp in a medium bowl and set aside. Place the peach halves cut side up in a baking dish about 1 inch apart.

Make the filling: Mash the reserved peach pulp with a fork into a paste. Add the crushed amaretti, sugar, ground almonds, and egg yolk and moisten with the amaretto liqueur. Mix till combined and then let the filling stand for 15 minutes. Preheat oven to 350 degrees.

Fill the center of each peach with some filling, distributing it evenly among all the peach halves. Dot each peach half with ¼ tablespoon of butter. Dissolve the sugar in the wine and pour in the bottom of the baking pan. Place in the preheated 350-degree oven and bake for 30 minutes. Serve warm or at room temperature with a drizzle of syrup from the bottom of the pan.

THE WINES OF EMILIA-ROMAGNA

Although Emilia-Romagna is a single region, it really reflects the traditions and histories of two separate entities. Emilia includes the provinces of Piacenza, Parma, Reggio-Emilia, Modena, Bologna, and Ferrara. Romagna encompasses all of the Adriatic coast, and is comprised of the southeast portion of the region, including the provinces of Ravenna, Forli, and Rimini.

In the appreciation for local wine, Emilia, the northwestern portion of the region, definitely favors Lambrusco. Whether *secco* (dry), *frizzante* (bubbly), or *amabile* (semisweet), it's a wine that is best when young and is drunk within the first year as a perfect balance to the rich food of the region. This wine made from the native Lambrusco grapes grown in the very fertile Po valley, and south of the river, is certainly the beloved king of the wines of Emilia.

The wines of Romagna, in the southeast area of the region, are made principally from the native Sangiovese grape that gives Romagna its favorite red wine. Trebbiano and Albana grapes produce the lighter whites; this last variety is the prized DOCG (*Denominazione di Origine Controllatae Garantita*). The history of Albana di Romagna begins in myth with the story of Galla Placida, the princess whose beauty so bedazzled the locals that they offered her their best sweet wine in an ample terracotta jug. The lovely lady was so taken by the deliciously smooth wine that she decreed that it be served from precious goblets as became the custom in the court of Ravenna. This wine comes in *secco* (dry), *amabile* (semisweet), *dolce* (sweet), and *passito,* which is a delicious dessert wine. The *passito* made from dried grapes concentrates the flavor and gives this lovely wine its fruity overtones. The Spumante Albana di Romagna is a beloved DOC sparkling wine of note.

Bologna, the capital of Emilia-Romagna, is known as "La Grassa" or "the fat"—a name that historically extolled the rich cooking of the region at a time when fat reflected the means and well-being of its people, who are still recognized as food connoisseurs. The regional wines, particularly the dry varieties, are enjoyed as an appropriate match for the region's rich cooking.

The hill wines of Emilia are also *frizzantini* or pleasingly frothy, although some of the wines of the Colli Piacentini, such as Ortugno white, could be *tranquillo*, not bubbly or *frizzante*. Gutturnio, a red wine, is a smooth blend of Barbera and Bonarda and is also produced as *tranquillo* and *frizzante*. The Colli Bolognesi produce Pignoletto, a crisp white wine that can be *amabile*, *secco*, or *frizzante*, and Barbera, a wonderfully hearty red. In the Colli di Parma in the foothills of the Appennini mountains, the major red wine produced is also Barbera, and among whites, the most typ-ical is Malvasia *secca* or *amabile*. Modena and Reggio-Emilia still produce Lambrusco wine from grapes that were known to the ancient Romans. Lambrusco remains the region's favorite sparkling wine.

GUIDE TO INGREDIENTS AND COOKING TECHNIQUES

INGREDIENTS

CURED MEATS:

Salumi (salted cured meats) are sold in *Salumerie* (specialty stores) in two forms: Whole cuts of meat such as **prosciutto** (cured ham), **culatello** (tender inner part of the ham), **coppa** (pork shoulder), **pancetta** (unsmoked bacon), **lardo** (pork fatback), and **guanciale** (pork cheek); or **insaccati** such as **salame, salsiccia** (sausages), **zampone** (pork leg boned and the skin stuffed, sewn, and cooked), **cotechino** (fat, sweet sausage), and **mortadella** (the cold cut typical of Bologna), all of which are minced, chopped, or ground meats which are seasoned, stuffed into casings and cooked, cured, or aged.

Affettati: The luscious *salumi* sliced for delectable antipasti.

Coppa: A specialty of Piacenza, this cured solid piece of marbled meat from the shoulder of the pork is dry salted, spiced, encased and air-dried and aged until rosy in color and delicately flavored with salt, pepper, and nutmeg with a touch of cloves or cinnamon.

Cotechino: Made famous in Cremona, this is a lightly cured sweet, thick pork sausage sold fresh, then cooked and served hot, traditionally accompanied by mashed potatoes and always by lentils on New Year's Day. In

Modena and Ferrara, *cotechino* is wrapped in a thin slice of beef and braised in wine (page 102).

Culatello: Made famous in Zibello, the meat is taken from the back leg of the pig and cured to give it fragrance, flavor, and moisture. This delectable meat is artisanally made with only a small portion of the leg muscle, and as a result is expensive but absolutely exquisite.

Guanciale: Cured pork jowls now being produced in the United States, it is perfection itself when bacon is too smoky and pancetta is too lean.

Lardo: Salt-cured pork fatback (not lard which in Italian is called ***sugna***), this is traditionally used for frying. The tasty, tender and flavorful white *lardo* is used in cooking and is also eaten as is in Italy. *Lardo* is the main ingredient in *condimento*, the spread that flavors *borlenghi*, a pancake-like flat bread, and *tigelle*, muffin-like little breads.

Mortadella: A smooth puree of ground pink pork meat spiced to perfection, studded with peppercorns and cubes of creamy *lardo* or fatback stuffed in a natural casing, cured for a few days in a cool dry place, and then cooked and cooled, *mortadella* is Bologna's gift to gastronomy bearing no resemblance to what is marketed as "bologna," a corruption of the sumptuous *Mortadella di Bologna*.

Pancetta: Italian bacon made from cured pork bellies that are rolled and dry cured rather than smoked.

Prosciutto di Parma: Salt-cured and air-dried, its production is highly regulated to produce a moist, sweet ham with unmistakable fragrance and flavor that marries well with fruit and the delicious flat, fried and baked breads of Emilia-Romagna for the ultimate antipasto.

Prosciutto ends: Italian grocers generally save the ends of the prosciutto and sell them inexpensively. These are a wonderful addition to soups, particularly minestrone with beans.

Salame: Dry-cured sausages made of coarsely ground pork meat with a good balance of fat and lean, delicately flavored with not one spice dominating the delicate flavor, then stuffed in a natural casing.

Salsiccie: Fresh pork sausages ready for frying, grilling, or adding to stuffings and ragus.

Zampone: Sausage meat stuffed in a pig's foot, lightly cured, always cooked and served hot. This specialty of Modena is not dissimilar to, and is spiced like, *cotechino*, which is considered its poor cousin.

OTHER INGREDIENTS:

Aceto Balsamico di Modena (balsamic vinegar from Modena): Another important export from Emilia-Romagna, this has become a household name as a condiment second to none. Aceto Commerciale is not aged and is used as a condiment for salads and cooking, whereas Aceto Tradizionale is aged for at least 12 years and Aceto Balsamico Stravecchio is at least 25 years old and is used sparingly as a rare treat to enhance the flavor of a variety of foods. Delicious drizzled on fruit and on Parmigiano-Reggiano cheese.

Amaretti di Saronno cookies: Imported from Italy and available all year, Amaretti di Saronno are tissue wrapped in pairs of two and marketed in familiar red tins. Delicious to accompany a cup of espresso, a glass of sweet wine, or a jigger of Amaretto di Saronno, they are also a staple ingredient in a variety of desserts. Four amaretti cookies weigh about one ounce. Local brands of amaretti cookies can be substituted, but Amaretti di Saronno are the best.

Amaretto di Saronno: A drink which calls itself "The World's Favorite Italian Liqueur" is a sweet almond-flavored cordial flavored with apricot kernel or almond oil which gives it the traditional bitter aftertaste. It is enjoyed as an after-dinner drink and also used as an ingredient in Italian desserts.

Battuto: *Battuto* is made by finely chopping onion, carrot, and celery all together, traditionally with a mezzaluna, the typical half-moon-shaped chopping knife with two handles that you move in a rocking motion either on a cutting board or using a special shallow bowl that fits the mezzaluna chopper. A chef's knife is a fine substitute for the mezzaluna.

Parmigiano-Reggiano cheese: Known as the king of cheeses, it's one of the signature foods of the region, known, renowned, and available all over the world. Save the rinds of the cheese to add to your soups. Add them at the beginning and cook with the soup to enrich and flavor the broth.

Porcini mushrooms (dried): Dried and graded according to quality, these mushrooms are soaked in hot water for 30 minutes, and drained from their flavorful soaking liquid which is reserved for cooking. The mushrooms are rinsed well to remove any grit, drained again and chopped before being added to a recipe.

Sauces: Cold sauces such as the ever popular *Salsa Verde* (Green Sauce) are served to accompany meats or fish. **Ragù** is a meat sauce that in Bologna is enriched at the end of cooking with heavy cream. Ragù is served on pasta and topped with what is playfully referred to as a "snowfall" of Parmigiano-Reggiano cheese. All sauces are used sparingly so as not to mask the goodness and flavor of the food they are dressing. In Emilia-Romagna, fresh pasta is unquestionably the star. The sauce is a light dressing that enhances but never overwhelms the *tagliatelle* (noodles).

Soffritto: The basis of most dishes is the *soffritto* which is made by cooking the *battuto* in butter, olive oil, or a combination of both with additions such as prosciutto, pancetta, or *guanciale* to further enrich and intensify the flavors.

Tagliatelle: *Tagliatelle* (noodles) are used in unique ways in the cooking of Emilia-Romagna. For *Bassotti*, a lovely savory dish, they are baked without having first been boiled, as is the norm, as they are for *torta Ferrarese* and *torta di Modena*, two typical desserts.

COOKING TECHNIQUES

Preparing dried beans:

1. Pick over the beans, wash and drain.
2. Soak overnight in plenty of cold water.
3. Drain the soaked beans, rinse, place in a pot, add cold water to cover plus 4 inches, bring water to a boil, lower the heat to a bare simmer, and cook for 1 to 1½ hours or until tender. Always add salt at the end to keep the skins from toughening.

Quick soaking method:

Place the beans in a pot, add cold water to cover plus 4 inches, bring to a boil, lower the heat, simmer for 10 minutes, turn off the heat and let stand for 1 hour. Continue with step 3 above.

Preparing lentils:

Lentils need no pre-soaking and very little cooking; long cooking breaks the skins.

1. Pick over the lentils for any hard pieces, wash, place in a pot, and cover with cold water plus 4 inches.
2. Bring to a boil, lower the heat to a bare simmer and cook for 5 minutes.
3. Turn off the heat and let stand for at least 2 hour or even overnight.
4. Strain the lentils, reserving the broth for soup.

Preparing dried porcini mushrooms:

Dried porcini mushrooms are the pride of Emilia-Romagna and the joy of their cooking.

1. Place the dried mushrooms in a bowl, cover with boiling water, and let soak for 30 minutes.
2. Drain through a fine strainer to remove any grit and reserve the liquid for soups, braises, or sauces.
3. Rinse the soaked mushrooms well. Chop and add to your recipe.

Preparing leeks:

Leeks require scrupulous cleaning to remove the dirt and sand between their leaves.

1. Trim the leeks by removing the roots and the tough green ends and rinse.
2. Cut into quarters up to but not through the root end, leaving the leeks attached at the root.

3. Soak the leeks in cold water swirling a few times to remove any sediment.
4. Rinse well under running water and cut or chop as desired.

Roasting, peeling, and preparing chestnuts: See pages 29 and 109.

COOKING COURSES IN EMILIA-ROMAGNA

Academia Barilla
Largo Piero Calamandrei 3/A
43100 Parma, Italy
Tel: 011 39 0521 264-060
www.academiabarilla.com

Internationally known cooking school in the heart of Parma
Courses and classes for professionals and food lovers alike to promote and develop Italian gastronomic culture
Includes classes, tastings, wine pairings, and tours

Ala d'Oro Hotel
Corso Matteotti 56
48022 Lugo, Ravenna
011-39- 0545- 22388
www.aladoro.it/nuovo/ristorante

Small classes
Courses taught by Chef Nadia Montuschi
Classes in noodle making and handmade pasta
Advanced classes in making *Piadine* and filled pasta

COOKING CLASSES IN NEW YORK CITY

Institute of Culinary Education
50 West 23rd Street
New York, NY 10010
212 847 0700
www.iceculinary.com

The Essentials of Emilia-Romagna Cooking
This Recreational Division Class is a hands-on class in which students cook under the direction of a chef/instructor, enjoy a buffet with wines of the region, and take home a packet of recipes. I teach classes at The Institute of Culinary Education and conduct guided walking tours of Arthur Avenue, the authentic little Italy of the Bronx.

RESOURCES IN THE UNITED STATES

Mike's Deli
Arthur Avenue Market
2344 Arthur Avenue
Bronx, NY 10458
(718) 295-5033
www.arthuravenue.com

Purveyors of imported and domestic salumi, cheeses, olive oils, and pasta. Catering. Serve their delicious food at Yankee Stadium. Also available on the Internet. They ship everywhere.

Monte Carmelo Gourmet
Arthur Avenue Market
2344 Arthur Avenue
Bronx, NY 10458
(718) 933-2295

Imported Italian products, large selection of dried pasta, biscotti, confetti, torrone, salted cod, anchovies, olive oils, and much more.

Teitel Brothers
2372 Arthur Avenue
Bronx, NY 1045
(718) 733-9400
www.teitelbros.com

An institution on Arthur Avenue for Italian specialty products of all types. Available on the Internet. They ship everywhere.

Tino's Delicatessen
2410 Arthur Avenue
Bronx, NY 10458
(718) 733-9879
www.tinosdeli.com

Excellent Italian domestic and imported products, catering, and a very welcoming place for eating and shopping.

Borgatti
632 East 187th Street
Bronx, NY 10458
(718) 298-6105

The Borgatti family has been making excellent fresh pasta and ravioli since the grandparents immigrated from Bologna and started the business in the Bronx in 1935. Their fresh egg, spinach, carrot, tomato, and whole wheat noodles are available every day except Sunday and Monday, together with tips and recipes.

Cerini
2334 Arthur Avenue
Bronx, NY 10458
(718) 584-3449

Large selection of Italian imports, espresso machines, coffee, gifts, and *bomboniere* (favors) for wedding and other celebrations.

Salumeria Biellese
378 8th Avenue
New York, NY 10001
www.salumeriabiellese.com

Excellent American made salumi: sausages, *culatello*. Available on the Internet. They ship everywhere.

Di Palo Dairy
200 Grand Street
New York, NY 10013
(212) 226-1033
www.dipalo.com

One of the most authentic Italian family-run stores in New York City's Greenwich Village with specialties from Italy, fresh cheeses, and traditional salumi made in America.

Williams-Sonoma
100 North Point
San Francisco, CA 94133
(800) 981-4466
www.williamssonoma.com

Cafasso's Fairway Market
1214 Anderson Avenue
Fort Lee, NJ 07024
(201) 224-7900
www.cafassosfairwaymkt.com

The best in Italian imported and domestic products, fresh produce, pre-pared foods, gift baskets, cheeses, and wines.

D'Artagnan
399-419 St. Paul Avenue
Jersey City, NJ 07306
(800) 327-8246
www.dartagnan.com

Specialty meats, game, duck, goose, venison, rabbit, Kobe-style wagyu, foie gras, buffalo, and charcuterie shipped everywhere.

Jerry's Gourmet
410 South Dean Street
Englewood, NJ 07631
(201) 871-7108
www.jerryshomemade.com

Excellent prepared foods, Italian imports, gift baskets, cookbooks, cheeses, and wines.

Salumi Artisan Cured Meats
309 Third Avenue South
Seattle, WA 98104

Armandino Batali, father of Chef Mario Batali, is a retired engineer who is exploiting his passion for food by producing and marketing excellent domestic artisanal cured meats.

La Quercia
400 Hakes Drive
Norwalk, Iowa
(515) 981-1625
www.laquercia.us

Genuine artisan dry cured meats made with no nitrates and nitrites, and 100% antibiotic free. Producers of artisan cured meats or salumi including prosciutto, *culaccia*, coppa, speck, pancetta, *guanciale*, and lardo.

Eataly
200 Fifth Avenue
New York, NY 10010
www.eataly.com

Eataly, a new gourmet destination in New York City patterned after the EATALY centers in Torino, Milano, and Bologna, Italy, is a delightful place for eating, shopping, or buying excellent prepared foods with a remarkable selection of fresh and filled pasta. Eataly-New York is the creation of Chef/Restauranteurs Mario Batali, Joe Bastianich, and Lidia Matticchio Bastianich.

BIBLIOGRAPHY

Battei, Antonio. *Dieci Verita' di Cucina Parmigiana*, Casa Editrice Battei, Parma 2005, ISBN 88-7883-092

Bertozzi, Alice. *Cucina dell'Emilia Romagna*, Giunti Editore S.p.A., Via Bolognese 165, 50139 Firenze, Italia; Via Dante 4, 20121 Milano, Italia, 2006, Prima Edizione: 2000, ISBN 88-440-3165-5

Boni, Ada. *Italian Regional Cooking*, E.P. Dutton & Co., Inc., New York 1969

Bugialli, Giuliano. *Parma, A Capital of Italian Gastronomy*, Academia Barilla Spa, Via Mantova 166-43100, Parma, 2005

Caggiano, Biba. *Biba's Taste of Italy*, William Morrow, Harper Collins Publishers Inc., 10 East 53rd Street, New York, NY 10022, 2001, ISBN 0-688-15815-3

De'Medici, Lorenza. *The Renaissance of Italian Cooking*, Fawcett Columbine, New York, Publisher: Ballantine Books, October 1989, ISBN 0-449-90364-8

Gioffrè, Rosalba and Marco Lanza. *Flavors of Italy, Emilia Romagna*, Time Life Books, Alexandria, Virginia, McRae Books Srl, 1999, ISBN 0-7370-0013-9

Geri Camporesi, Carla. *Tempo di Castagne – Chestnut Time*, Maria Pacini Fazzi, Editore, 55100 Lucca-Piazza San Romano, 16, 1993, ISBN 88-7246-113-8

Maculan, Guerrino. *Le Ricette Colori e Sapori in Cucina di Guerrino*, Casa Editrice Battei, Parma 2004

Malerba, Giulia, coordinamento editoriale. *Le Migliori Ricette dei Lettori della Gazzetta di Parma*, Via Mazzini 6, 43100 Parma, Via Bordoni 8, 20124 Milano, May 2007, Tipolitografia di Parma, ISBN 88-6154-016-3

Marchesi, Gustavo. *Buon Appetito Maestro, a Tavola con Giuseppe Verdi*, Casa Editrice Luigi Battei, Parma 2001

Martini, Fosca. *Romagna in Bocca*, Editrice "Il Vespro", Via Degli Orti 41, Palermo, 1977

Rossetto Kasper, Lynne. *The Splendid Table*, William Morrow and Company, Inc., New York, 1350 Avenue of The Americas, New York, NY 10019, 1992, ISBN 0-688-08963-1

Sartoni, Monica Cesari and Allessandro Molinari Pradelli. *La Cucina Bolognese*, Newton & Compton editori, Roma, casella postale 6214, ottobre 2001, ISBN 88-8289-644-X

Sidoli, Richard Camillo. *The Cooking of Parma*, Rizzoli International Publications, Inc. 300 Park Avenue South, New York, NY 10010, 1996

ITALIAN RECIPE NAME INDEX

INDEX

ABOUT THE AUTHOR

GIOVANNA BELLIA LA MARCA was born in Italy came to the United States at the age of 10. She has kept her love for Sicilian and Italian cooking alive through many trips to Italy. Retired after a 20-year career as an art and Italian teacher, she taught cooking classes at the Institute of Culinary Education in New York City and led culinary tours of Arthur Avenue in the Bronx. She also devotes herself to writing, cooking, entertaining, and traveling with her family and hosts a popular YouTube cooking show "Kitchen on the Cliff." La Marca is also author of *Sicilian Feasts* and *Language and Travel Guide to Sicily*, both published by Hippocrene Books. She resides in Cliffside Park, New Jersey.

Also by

Giovanna Bellia LaMarca

SICILIAN FEASTS:
Illustrated Edition

"… a superbly presented collection of rich, lip-smacking treats offering a festival of taste and exploration for adventurous dining."

—*The Midwest Book Review*

Now available in an illustrated edition with new recipes and color photos!

Sicilian Feasts was born out of the author's love for her native Sicily. Giovanna Bellia La Marca uses simple methods and readily available ingredients to teach the straightforward and delectable everyday cooking of Sicily. The history, customs, and folklore, as well as the flavorful and varied cuisine of her beautiful Mediterranean island are well represented in these recipes and stories.

A chapter on Sicilian staples that fit the parameters of the Mediterranean Diet, such as "Winter Caponata," "Kohlrabi Soup," Kale with Fava Beans," and "Pears Cooking in Wine," showcase vegetables, leafy greens, legumes, nuts and honey—foods on which Sicilians have thrived for thousands of years. Throughout the book, vegetarian and vegan recipes are marked for readers.

Sicilian Feasts offers more than 180 recipes, along with menus for holidays, notes on ingredients, lists of suppliers, an introduction to the Sicilian language, and a glossary of food terms in Sicilian, Italian, and English. Illustrations demonstrate special techniques.

ISBN 978-0-7818-1433-1

Available in hardcover and e-book format